BLOWBACK

A CAUTIONARY TALE

BLOWBACK

HOW THE WEST F*CKED UP
THE MIDDLE EAST

MICHAEL LUDERS

First published in Great Britain in 2017 by Old Street Publishing Ltd
Yowlestone House, Tiverton, Devon EX16 8LN
www.oldstreetpublishing.co.uk

ISBN 978-1-910400-55-5

Copyright © Michael Lüders

Translation copyright © Old Street Publishing
(with grateful acknowledgement to Katharina Becker)

10 9 8 7 6 5 4 3 2 1

A CIP catalogue record for this title is available from the British Library.

Printed and bound by CPI Group (UK) Ltd, Croydon, CR0 4YY

When everybody's thinking the same thing, I start having doubts.
Stefan Hell, Nobel Prizewinner for Chemistry, 2014

CONTENTS

Introduction

'Sow the wind, reap the whirlwind'

When I told a friend in Budapest the idea for this book, he understood it in his own way: 'How the Americans and the British fucked up the Middle East and happily continue to do so.' Essentially, he was right. *Blowback* is an attempt to hold to account Western policy, which claims to act from moral principles but again and again leaves nothing but scorched earth in its wake. The main protagonists are the United States of America and its closest ally, the United Kingdom, but since 9/11 they have been joined by other European countries.

No one who wants to understand today's conflicts, including the rise of Islamic State, the nuclear wranglings with Iran or the slaughter in Syria, can afford to ignore the influence of Western policy on the region since the end of World War II. The West is not the sole culprit of the Middle East's misfortunes, but the basic pattern of Western intervention in the Arab-Islamic world has scarcely changed since the toppling of Mohammed Mossadegh, the democratically elected Prime Minister of Iran, in 1953.

Ever since this 'original sin' of intervention, the West has relied upon a crude division of opposing parties into good and evil. Once a state, a non-state entity (Hamas, Hezbollah), or a leader has been branded 'evil', the process of demonisation is completed only too willingly by thinktanks and the media. The comparison with Hitler is an especially beloved tactic – from which it naturally follows that a willingness to negotiate is mere cover for appeasement, collaboration, and the betrayal of 'Western values'.

The first to be thus demonised as a 'second Hitler' was Mohammed Mossadegh, who in 1951 nationalised the Iranian oil industry (previously under British control) and two years later paid the price with a coup sponsored by the British and American secret services. Then came President Nasser of Egypt, who dared to nationalise the Suez Canal in 1956, thereby incurring the rage of the British and French investors. The most recent trio to join the ever-lengthening list of reincarnated Hitlers are Saddam Hussein, the ex-President of Iran, Mahmoud Ahmadinedjad of Iran, and the Syrian President, Bashar al-Assad, with Russia's Putin on the reserve list.

Naturally, absolute Evil must have its counterpart: selfless Good. That's us Westerners. We stand for Freedom, Democracy and Human Rights. Whenever they can, Western politicians stress values, and avoid talking about interests. As they despatch their warships or their bombers, they like to give the impression that they are simply implementing a global program of democratisation and aid. Under the banner of such noble motives, the mistakes, oversights, lies and crimes that have, in the Arab-Islamic world alone, cost hundreds of thousands of lives, can be generously overlooked. After all, surely the good guys have the right to punish the baddies, for example by sanctions (with the attendant if unspoken hope that they will bring down said 'evil' regime).

Baddies, of course, can come and go as swiftly as sanctions. Those imposed on China after the Tiananmen Square massacre were quietly lifted by Washington as the economic ties between the two super-powers deepened, with Iran and Russia taking on the villain's mantle (and the sanctions). The election of Donald Trump as the 45th President of the United States is reshuffling the pack once again.

The self-appointed good guys like to believe in their own moral superiority – because they push for freedom in the Ukraine, say, or for human rights in Iran – but the chief purpose of their interventions is geopolitical: to destroy or weaken their opponents. And they continue to believe in the success of their policies – that, for instance, their sanctions forced the Mullahs to negotiate about Iran's atomic program. Yet this is only partially true. Sooner or later, the West was always going to have to come to an arrangement with Iran, the unavoidable central power in the region.

There is no shortage of evidence that the economic and military resources of the West are stretched to their limits, that American power is on the wane, and that we can no longer simply enforce our wishes upon an increasingly multi-polar world. Yet most politicians continue to act according to the Cold War premise that 'West is Best'. How else can we explain the ongoing preference for confrontation over cooperation? Why else do they show so little readiness to learn from past mistakes? Has the 'War on Terror' defeated Islamist extremism in Afghanistan? In Syria? Iraq? If drone attacks are included, the United States has intervened militarily in seven predominantly Muslim countries since 2001: Afghanistan, Iraq, Somalia, Yemen, Pakistan, Libya and Syria. In which of these states have the lives of the inhabitants improved as a result? Where have stability and security emerged? Is there, in fact, a single Western military intervention that has not resulted in chaos, dictatorship and fresh waves of violence? Without the fall of Saddam Hussein at the hands of a US-led 'coalition of the willing' and the ensuing devastation of the Iraqi state under an ill-informed and sectarian occupation force, would Islamic State exist today?

The region from Algeria to Pakistan represents an almost

unbroken arc of crisis, plagued by wars, state collapse, stagnation and violence. The causes are numerous, but two stand out. First is the long-standing inability – or reluctance – of the local ruling elites to serve any but their own partisan interests. The slightest opposition is violently suppressed, until at last tensions boil over, as during the Arab Spring revolts in Egypt and Libya. The resulting power vacuum is then filled by a chaotic assortment of generals, militias, and warlords, of clans and tribes, of religious and ethnic groups. Fragmentation, self-destruction and barbarity follow. This is an environment in which jihadi groups thrive, using the Koran and the general distress of the population to justify all forms of arbitrary violence, conquest and terror.

The second cause is the baneful influence of the West since colonial times, not least the arbitrary 'lines in the sand' drawn through the Middle East by Britain and France after World War I. In the 1950s, though, a new power became dominant in the region. The consequences of Washington's interventions – above all of the Tehran coup in 1953 – are still being felt today, even if we in the West have conveniently forgotten them, or overlaid them with the myth of a benevolent, 'irreplaceable' superpower.

Let us then start with the past, in order better to understand the present: in Iran.

COUP IN TEHRAN: THE 'ORIGINAL SIN'

The coup against the democratically elected Prime Minister of Iran, Mohammed Mossadegh, had been minutely planned over months of preparation. The CIA and the British Secret Service, MI6, had left nothing to chance. The aim was clearly stated in the title of a recently released CIA document from 1953:

CAMPAIGN TO INSTALL PRO-WESTERN GOVERNMENT IN IRAN AUTHORITY

TARGET

Prime Minister Mossadeq and his government

OBJECTIVES

Through legal, or quasi-legal, methods, to effect the fall of the Mossadeq government; and

To replace it with a pro-western government under the Shah's leadership, with Zahedi as its Prime Minister.

CIA ACTION

Plan of action was implemented in four phases:

1. [Censored] (...) to strengthen the Shah's will to exercise his constitutional power and to sign those decrees necessary to effect the legal removal of Mossadeq as Prime Minister;

2. Welded together and co-ordinated the efforts of those political factions in Iran who were antagonistic towards Mossadeq, including the powerfully influential clergy, to

gain the support and backing of any legal action taken by the Shah to accomplish Mossadeq's removal;

3.[Censored] (...) disenchant the Iranian population with the myth of Mossadeq's patriotism, by exposing his collaboration with Communists and his manipulation of constitutional authority to serve his own personal ambitions for power;

[Censored] (...) Simultaneously, conducted a 'war of nerves' against Mossadeq designed to reveal to Mossadeq and to the general populace that increased economic aid would not be forthcoming and that the U.S. viewed with alarm Mossadeq's policies:

a. A series of public statements by high U.S. officials, implying that there was little hope that Mossadeq could expect increased U.S. aid;

b. U.S. press and magazine articles which were critical of him and his methods; and

c. [Censored] (...) absence of the American ambassador, lending credence to the impression that the U.S. had lost confidence in Mossadeq and his government (...)[1]

Exactly sixty years later to the day, on 19 August 2013, the National Security Archive of George Washington University published the CIA documents, obtained under the Freedom of Information Act, on the internet – at least those not still classified as 'top secret'. They make eye-opening reading, and bear alarming witness to the cold-blooded professionalism with

---

1 National Security Archive, George Washington University, Electronic Briefing Book No. 435, 19 August 2013. Document 2: CIA, Summary 'Campaign to install pro-western government in Tehran', draft of internal history of the coup, undated.

which the CIA engineered the overthrow of another country's elected government. For the first time, the CIA was forced to admit in public that the American secret services had played a leading role in the Iranian *coup d'état*.

This is not just a matter of historical interest. Throughout the recent 12-year battle of wills over Iran's nuclear program, the 1953 coup was the 'elephant in the room'. For Iranians, the question was as much about whether the Americans could be trusted to stick to the deal and respect Iranian sovereignty as it was about the deal itself. Would the US really back off in return for a reduction in uranium stocks and enrichment facilities? Or would they continue to push for regime change even after extracting such concessions?

President Obama's famous speech in Cairo in 2009 showed how vividly the toppling of Mossadegh – which cut short the brief Iranian experiment in democracy, first ushering in the Shah's dictatorship, then the 1979 Islamic Revolution – is still remembered today. In that speech, Obama admitted that 'in the middle of the Cold War, the United States played a role in the overthrow of a democratically elected Iranian government.' A single sentence, deliberately vague, but one that resonated throughout the Arab and Muslim world.

Riches Beyond Our 'Wildest Dreams'

To this day, the British government's role in the coup remains officially unacknowledged. In 1978, high-ranking British officials persuaded Washington not to make public documents which would be 'very embarrassing' for London. In an article in the *Daily Telegraph* in 2009, written in response to Obama's Cairo speech, Foreign Minister Jack Straw did concede that during the 20th century there had been many 'interferences' by Great Britain in Iranian affairs, though the Foreign Office remained non-committal, stating that they could 'neither confirm nor deny' participation in the coup.

One reason for this coyness might be that the original idea actually came from London. Since its beginnings in 1909, the British had enjoyed a monopoly on the Iranian oil industry. In 1935, the Anglo-Persian Oil Company became the Anglo-Iranian Oil Company (AIOC), which in 1953 sired British Petroleum (BP), still a massive global player today. In the decades before World War II, around £800 million of oil profits flowed into Britain, while Iran, the owner of the oil, received just £105 million. It was not for nothing that Churchill characterised the AIOC as 'a prize from fairyland beyond our wildest dreams.'

Iran was *de facto* a British colony. In the major oil-producing city of Abadan in the Persian Gulf, an apartheid system was in place, with Iranians barred from senior management positions, and segregated in low-quality 'native' housing. Poor working conditions led repeatedly to protests and strikes, which were violently put down. By the end of the 1940s a political protest movement had formed, and a group of parliamentarians was demanding the right to renegotiate the oil exploration contracts with Great Britain. Their spokesman was the French- and Swiss-educated lawyer Mohammed Mossadegh. He and his comrades founded the National Front, whose mission was to end to British overrule and challenge the autocratic rule of the Shah. Their demands included press freedom, free and fair elections, and a constitutional monarchy.

Some decades earlier, the Shah had himself seized power by violent means. In 1921, as an officer in the elite Cossack brigade of the Persian Army, Reza Khan led a successful revolt against the

Qajar dynasty which had ruled since 1796. On being crowned Shah in 1926, he assumed the title *Pahlavi*, in reference to the language spoken in the glory days of Persia's Sassanid Empire (224–621 AD). In 1941, the Allies forced him to abdicate, owing to his ties with Nazi Germany, and he was succeeded by his son, Mohammed Reza. The corrupt electoral system meant that the new Shah could count on a loyal group of supporters in parliament, whom the British cultivated as a bulwark against the rise of Mossadegh's National Front.

Nevertheless, after the parliamentary elections of 1950, the National Front became one of the strongest parties, and submitted a proposal to the AIOC for a fairer distribution of oil revenues. The AIOC refused point blank to negotiate, provoking strikes and protests across the country. A large swathe of the population now went further, and began to demand the wholesale nationalisation of the oil industry. The National Front, enraged by British intransigence, backed them, as did a majority of the highly influential clergy.

When Mohammed Mossadegh became Prime Minister in March 1951, his opponents were quick to recognise the threat. The British government had no intention of ceasing its lucrative exploitation of Iranian resources: some 90 percent of all the oil traded in Europe at that time came from the Abadan refinery. The US government under President Truman were more ambivalent: they shared Mossadegh's desire, albeit for different reasons, to see the back of the Shah's crumbling regime. Consequently, the nationalisation of the Iranian oil industry at first triggered no great irritation across the Atlantic. Indeed, *Time* magazine featured Mossadegh on the front cover of their 7 January 1952 edition as their 'Man of the Year', praising him as a courageous reformer.

Winston Churchill, now Prime Minister again, and his Foreign Minister Anthony Eden, could only remove Mossadegh with Washington's approval and support. Their chance came in 1953, when Eisenhower became President. The planned putsch now became an American-led affair. Truman, a Democrat, had warned that a violent Western intervention in Iranian affairs would bring 'disaster to the free world', but the Republicans saw in Mossadegh above all a communist, and in his program of nationalisation a dangerous precedent.

A Dangerous Madman

The 1953 coup showcases the pattern that the US and its allies still adhere to when they want to bring down a foreign regime: first, demonise the enemy, then send in the troops. Eden repeatedly likened Mossadegh to Hitler, while a CIA document describes him in terms which re-appear almost word for word in relation to Saddam Hussein, Gaddafi and Assad. Mossadegh was one of the most 'mercurial, maddening, adroit, and provocative' leaders with whom they had ever dealt.[2] He had, it was alleged, whipped up the fury of Iranian people against the British, by branding them as 'evil' and self-serving exploiters of their country.

The key figure in the joint operation – code-named 'TPA-JAX' in the US, 'Boot' by the British – was CIA man Kermit Roosevelt, grandson of former US President, Theodore Roosevelt. He supervised the coup, following the plan of action cited

---

2 National Security Archive, George Washington University, Electronic Briefing Book No. 435, 19 August 2013. Document 4: CIA, History, 'Zendebad, Shah!': The Central Intelligence Agency and the Fall of Iranian Prime Minister Mohammed Mossadeq, August 1953, Scott A. Koch, June 1998

above, and bolstering it with several additional measures whose details remain censored. For example, he distributed millions of dollars, not just to the Shah's loyal supporters, but to soldiers and mobs, who obliged by creating the violence and chaos on the streets needed to camouflage the putsch. Meanwhile, dozens of journalists were bribed to tar Mossadegh as an agent of the Soviet Union, and his former Interior Minister, Fazlollah Zahedi, was primed to oust him.

The CIA divided the day of the operation, 19 August, into four phases:

Phase 1: The Great Demonstration 06.00 am–10.30 am
   Four bands of 'ruffians' were paid by the organisers of the coup to demonstrate, under the leadership of nationally popular wrestler, Shaban 'Bimokh' (no-brains) Jafari. They gathered in the bazaar, and other sections of Southern Tehran, before marching northwards.

Phase 2: The Injection of Armed Forces and Undercover Agents 10.00 am–15.00 pm
   The Ministries of Propaganda, Foreign Affairs and Interior Affairs were occupied, along with municipal buildings such as the Town Hall, the telegraph office and the HQs of both the civil and the military police. Meanwhile, the offices of newspapers and the HQs of various political parties were attacked and set ablaze.

Phase 3: Tank Deployment and Entrapment 05.00 am–14.30 pm
   Pro-Shah forces gained control of some 24 tanks during the course of the day and used them to seize key parts of the city centre.

Phase 4: Attaining Targets 14.00 pm–19.00 pm

Between 14.00 and 16.00, tanks secured the main radio station for the insurgents, whilst anti-Mossadegh forces converged on his house in the west of the city. Between 16.00 and 17.00, Zahedi addressed the Iranian people, via the radio station, as their new Prime Minister, and by 19.00 Mossadegh had been forced to flee the mob by escaping over the walls of his house.

Mossadegh was allowed to flee so that he could later be portrayed as a coward. He was sentenced to three years' imprisonment in a show trial and placed under house arrest until the end of his life in 1967.

In this squalid drama, Mossadegh cuts a tragic figure. He was an advocate of parliamentary democracy, and an admirer of Mahatma Gandhi and Abraham Lincoln. Today, in fact, we would say that he shared 'Western values'. They did him little good. On 16 August 1953, three days before the successful coup, his supporters had foiled an initial attempt. Mossadegh, assuming that the British government were behind it, but refusing to believe that the Americans could be involved, asked the US ambassador for help. The ambassador advised him to restore calm and order, which he attempted to do by outlawing protests by the communist Tudeh party.

After the coup, the Shah returned from his brief exile. The National Front and the Tudeh party were both banned, and two ministers were executed, along with numerous Communists. 'I owe my throne to God, my people, my army – and you,' said the Shah to Kermit Roosevelt, the mastermind of the coup (at least according to Roosevelt's own memoirs).

For the next twenty-six years, Washington felt the gratitude of the Shah markedly more than his subjects. He allowed Iran to become a military support base for the Americans on the southern borders of the Soviet Union, and Israel's most important ally in the region. Tehran became Washington's policeman, countering and quelling nationalist and leftist movements throughout the Islamic world. A new international oil consortium was founded for the benefit of American exploration companies, which held 40% of the shares, the same proportion as BP. With bitter irony, the new contract guaranteed 50% of oil revenues to Iran, a figure Mossadegh might himself have been content with.

The Shah set in motion a top-down modernization of the country, whose main beneficiaries were the country's tiny upper-class elite and foreign corporations. Over the decades, his rule came to rest increasingly on the feared secret service, SA-VAK, whose agents received training from America and Israel. During the 1970s, the bazaar (the traditional backbone of the Iranian economy) and the mosques grew into strongholds of opposition under the leadership of the charismatic Ayatollah Khomeini, who, initially from exile in Iraq, then from Paris, led and directed the resistance movement, until it broke out in the 1979 revolution.

First Coup, then Revolution

The Islamic Revolution which propelled Khomeini to power was a delayed response to the 1953 coup. Anglo-American arrogance had brutally snuffed out a promising parliamentary democracy, substituting the dictatorship of a man viewed by the West as a reliable partner, but who blocked every attempt to construct a civil society within his own land. Spending vast sums on mega-projects (including, from 1957, a nuclear program) in a bid to 'modernise'

13

the country, the Shah failed to improve the lot of the vast majority of his subjects, who lived in rural poverty and sprawling urban slums. Shiite Islam became a receptacle of accumulated dissatisfaction, which ultimately proved more powerful than the Shah, the urban elites, and even the dreaded SAVAK.

No 1953 coup, no Islamic Revolution. A simple point, but one America finds hard to swallow. Obama's solitary sentence of self-criticism during his 2009 Cairo speech was swiftly followed by one of self-justification: 'Since the Islamic Revolution, Iran has played a role in acts of hostage-taking and violence against US troops and civilians.' The subtext: *now we're quits*.

Americans and Europeans rarely ask themselves whether the widespread popular loathing of Western policy in the Middle East might actually be justified. In America, it is the 444-day hostage situation endured by US diplomats in Tehran from 1979 to 1981 that is seen as the outrage of the era, rather than the self-serving and illegal removal of Mossadegh three decades before. The anti-American sentiment of the Khomeini regime is explained away as a by-product of fanatical Islam, and battle-cries like 'Death to America' or 'Death to Israel' are seen as irrational expressions of religious hatred rather than an understandable reaction to unwarranted US interference and support of the Shah.

Shortly after he took office in 1953, half a year before the coup in Iran, President Eisenhower asked the National Security Council why most people outside the Western hemisphere were antipathetic towards American policies. The CIA could have told him it was *blowback* – the term the agency uses to describe how secret operations in other countries often rebound on their originator.

Without the 1953 coup, there would have been no Islamic Revolution. This message cannot be hammered home enough.

The putsch against Mossadegh was the 'original sin', and its effects are still being felt today. Since Khomeini came to power, Iran has been regarded as an enemy by the West, where Islam has replaced Communism as the bogeyman of preference. From 1979 on, the US, Europe, Israel and the Gulf states have been pursuing, with varying levels of intensity, openly or covertly, the goal of limiting and weakening Iran as a regional power – and if possible, of regime change.

Of course, it is not only in the West that the Mullahs are feared and loathed. Their ruthlessness during the first years of the Islamic Republic, when tens of thousands of the regime's opponents were liquidated, combined with a harsh internal climate of repression and a foreign policy that has alienated neighbours, have not made them popular figures within their own country. Yet we should not forget that it was with the Iranian Revolution that Islamic fundamentalism experienced its major breakthrough, in countries from Morocco to Indonesia, at the expense of secular, nationalist and pro-Western movements. Aided and abetted (if unconsciously) by the CIA, MI6, and Kermit 'Kim' Roosevelt, Khomeini and his revolution represent the *Big Bang* of political Islam.[3]

---

3 This despite the fact that Iran is a Shiite country, while most Muslims are Sunnis.

ENDGAME IN THE HINDU KUSH: WASHINGTON AND RIYADH, MIDWIVES OF AL-QAIDA

The Islamic Revolution in Iran was not the only momentous global event of 1979. It was also the year in which Soviet troops entered Afghanistan. Ever since Alexander the Great, the mountainous territory in the Hindu Kush had attracted conquerors. In the 19th century, Afghanistan became the focus of competing colonial attentions from Russia and Britain. After 1979 it became once again a geopolitical battlefield, this time with the Soviet Union ranged against the US, Saudi Arabia and Pakistan.

Even today, Afghanistan appears archaic: the slow rhythm of life in the countryside; the customs scarcely changed for centuries; the economy still largely a subsistence one. Amanullah Khan, the first king after independence in 1919, tried to implement a program of modernisation and to promote trade with the rest of the world. Following the model of Atatürk's reforms in Turkey, he broke with tradition by introducing compulsory education and allowing girls to go to school. These measures, however, provoked nationwide resistance, and finally led to his demise in 1929.

The next would-be 'moderniser' was Mohammed Daoud Khan, Amanullah's great-nephew, who seized power in 1973 in a bloodless coup, abolishing the monarchy, and declaring himself President. Yet he too was faced with the thankless task of leading Afghanistan out of the Middle Ages with no solid block of support outside the country's tiny middle and upper classes. At first, he had the backing of the Communist People's Democratic Party of Afghanistan, the only secular and cross-ethnic party of any size, whose constituency came mostly from the Kabul intelligentsia. In 1978, however, backed by the Soviets, the Communists liquidated Daoud and assumed power themselves. Like their predecessor, they tried to implement a modernisation and literacy program, but came up against bitter opposition from the rural population, from local and regional leaders, and from the clergy. Armed resistance to the 'infidels' spread through the country, threatening to ignite a civil war. To prevent the situation getting out of hand, and to keep Afghanistan within Moscow's sphere of influence, the Soviet army invaded in Christmas 1979In doing so, they fell headlong into a skilfully-laid CIA trap, whose aim was nothing less than the collapse of the Soviet Union.

Regrets?

One of the architects of this Machiavellian scheme – which, as we shall see, sowed the seeds of the 9/11 terror attacks – was Zbigniew Brzezinski, at that time National Security Advisor to US President Jimmy Carter. In January 1997, in an interview with the French magazine *Le Nouvel Observateur*, Brzezinski, perhaps keen to blow his own trumpet, gave an extraordinary insight into the workings of power:

> Interviewer: The former director of the CIA, Robert Gates, stated in his memoirs that the American intelligence services began to aid the mujahideen in Afghanistan six months before the Soviet intervention. In this period, you were the national security advisor to President Carter. You

therefore played a key role in this affair. Is this correct?

Brzezinski: Yes. According to the official version of history, CIA aid to the mujahideen began during 1980, that is to say, after the Soviet army invaded Afghanistan on 24 December 1979. But the reality, closely guarded until now, is completely otherwise: indeed, it was on 3 July 1979 that President Carter signed the first directive for secret aid to the opponents of the pro-Soviet regime in Kabul. And that very day, I wrote a note to the president in which I explained to him that *in my opinion this aid was going to induce a Soviet military intervention.* [Author's note: italics added throughout.]

Interviewer: Despite this risk, you were an advocate of this covert action. But perhaps you yourself desired this Soviet entry into the war and were looking for a way to provoke it?

Brzezinski: It wasn't quite like that. *We didn't push the Russians to intervene, but we knowingly increased the probability that they would.*

Interviewer: When the Soviets justified their intervention by asserting that they intended to fight against secret US involvement in Afghanistan, nobody believed them. However, there was an element of truth in this. You don't regret any of this today?

Brzezinski: Regret what? That secret operation was an excellent idea. It had the effect of *drawing the Russians into the Afghan trap* and you want me to regret it? The day that the Soviets officially crossed the border, *I wrote to President Carter, essentially: 'We now have the opportunity of giving to the USSR its Vietnam War.'* Indeed, for almost ten years, Moscow had to carry on a war that was unsustainable for the regime, a conflict that bought about the demoralization and finally the break-up of the Soviet empire.

Interviewer: And neither do you regret having supported Islamic fundamentalism, which has given arms and advice to future terrorists?

Brzezinski: What is more important in world history? The Taliban or the collapse of the Soviet empire? Some agitated Muslims or the liberation of Central Europe and the end of the Cold War?[4]

Saudi Arabia and Pakistan were the US's most important allies in the fight against the Kremlin. After the Soviet invasion, seeking to redress the regional balance of power after the Shiite Revolution in Iran, the House of Saud proclaimed a Holy War – albeit one at a safe distance, and in close cooperation with its entirely un-Islamic American ally. Afghanistan became a battleground once again, with jihad against the Soviet occupation (1979–1989) working as an instrument both of Saudi self-assertion and Cold War power-play, as well as a beacon to the dispossessed

---

4 Translated from the French by William Blum and David N. Gibbs. This translation was published in Gibbs, 'Afghanistan: The Soviet Invasion in Retrospect', *International Politics* 37, no. 2, 2000, pp. 241-242. The original French version appeared in *"Les Révélations d'un Ancien Conseilleur de Carter: 'Oui, la CIA est Entrée en Afghanistan avant les Russes...'"* *Le Nouvel Observateur* [Paris], January 15-21, 1998, p. 76.

of the Muslim world. Liberally funded by Saudi Arabia, radical Islamists from Algeria to Pakistan streamed in their thousands to Afghanistan, where they fought as *mujahideen*, warriors of faith, against the communist unbelievers.

Saudi Arabia – The Original 'Islamic State'

At first sight the alliance between Washington and Riyadh may have seemed, as Brzezinski put it, a 'brilliant idea': the Saudis as stooges of American and Western interests, unwitting pawns in a grand plan to bring down the Berlin Wall. But it came at a high price: 15 of the 19 terrorists involved in 9/11 hailed orginally from Saudi Arabia. The brutality of Islamic State, too, has its ideological roots in the Wahhabi strain of Sunni Islam followed in Saudi Arabia, while the fundamental Sunni–Shia conflict continues to find expression in violence and terror from Lebanon to Iraq to Pakistan. To understand the connections, a deeper look at the history is needed.

In Saudi Arabia, Islam is the state religion; or, to be more precise, an arch-conservative, theocratic branch of the faith called Wahhabism. Its founder was the revivalist preacher Mohammed Ibn Abd al-Wahhab (d. 1792) who followed the medieval theologian Ibn Taymiyya in demanding the union of state and religion, as well as strict adherence to the fundamentals of the Islamic faith as he understood them.

The Saudi state emerged in 1932, but the modern history of the country dates to the late 18th century, when al-Wahhab's supporters allied themselves with the ascendant al-Saud tribe, to their mutual advantage. From then on, the Wahhabis benefited from the support of a strong tribal dynasty, while the al-Saud tribe obtained religious legitimacy for its own claim to hegemony over all rival tribes. Wahhabist doctrine still underpins life in a country where, for example, women are not permitted to drive cars or set foot outside without being covered in the *abaya* gown. Wahhabi Islam also bans prayers with any reference to saints or the deceased; it forbids pilgrimages to tombs, graves or mausoleums, as well as any public commemoration of the prophet Mohammed's birthday. It even bans grave stones. All such acts are viewed as distractions from the pure worship of Allah.

Without the alliance with the al-Sauds, this early variant of Islamic fundamentalism might today be seen as an insignificant and short-lived sectarian footnote. But with Saudi oil wealth behind it, Wahhabism has been able to penetrate into the furthest corners of the Islamic world, to suppress reform movements, and to exert influence on the global political stage.

In the Wahhabi state, all difference of opinion is denounced as blasphemy. No doubt fear keeps many in line – those who stray are liable to have their property confiscated, their wives and daughters violated, their lives taken. As for Shia Muslims, Alawites, followers of the mystical Sufi traditions: no matter how pious, all such non-Wahhabi strains of Islam are deemed as godless as the Christian or the atheist, and deserving of the same fate.

The Womb of Fanaticism

Ideologically, there is precious little to choose between Saudi Islam and that of the assorted branches of Islamic State and al-Qaida. In the end it boils down to a question of loyalties. In Saudi Arabia these are to the King, head of the ruling House of Saud; in the Islamic State, they are to the self-appointed Caliph, a 45-year-old Iraqi known as Abu Bakr al-Baghdadi; in al-Qaida's case, they were to Osama bin Laden. Fanatical Islamists of all stripes practise *takfir*, whereby opponents are declared unbelievers and may be legitimately murdered. IS and al-Qaida might prefer to dissociate themselves from the decadent opulence of the Saudi kingdom, but Saudi-funded Wahhabism was the womb in which they were formed.

Violent conquest is central to the history of the Saudi Wahhabis. In the 1790s they took over region after region of the area now known as Saudi Arabia, offering conquered tribes the stark choice between death or submission. They elevated conflict into a sacred act – jihad – and its soldiers, the jihadis, into heroes who would gain instant entry to Paradise by perishing in battle. In 1801, presumably inspired by such beliefs, a force of warrior Wahhabis attacked Kerbala in Iraq, a town sacred to the Shia Muslims. They massacred around 5,000 people, including women and children, led thousands into slavery, and destroyed several Shiite tombs, including that of Imam Hussein, the murdered grandson of the Prophet Mohammed.

In 1803, they took Mecca, burning to the ground the old town, with its tombs and shrines (including even the grave of the Prophet) and obliterated centuries' worth of Islamic architectural history around the Great Mosque. The Ottoman Empire, which had claimed sovereignty over the city since 1517, reacted by pushing the attackers back as far as Riyadh. But they returned in 1924, on a scale so formidable that Mecca's defenders simply fled, leaving their cannons behind. Chroniclers report that the air was filled with a strange humming, even before the Saudi warriors came in sight. When the city's defenders saw that a phalanx of holy warriors was approaching, chanting as though in a trance the word *Janna* (paradise), they were filled with panic. The more recent advance of the armies of Islamic State was strikingly similar. The jihadis' crusading zeal and their readiness to die sent regular soldiers in Iraq and Syria fleeing in their tens of thousands, without so much as firing a shot.

After the victory, Abdulaziz ibn Saud (1880–1953), the founder of Saudi Arabia, had 40,000 opponents of Wahhabism executed, and his supporters plundered the treasure of the Mosque of the Prophet in Medina, burning all the books, including copies of the Koran, that they found there. They forbade music and flowers, tobacco and coffee. Under threat of death, men were forced to grow beards, women to wear the veil and to keep themselves out of public view.

Today the Taliban, al-Qaida and Islamic State all go about things in much the same way. Since the oil money began flowing in the 1930s, Riyadh has vigorously promoted the spread of Wahhabism throughout the Islamic world: the aim is to 'wahhabise' Islam itself. Billions of dollars have been spent in the quest to reduce the many currents of Islam to one 'faith', whose earthly custodians are the al-Saud rulers. Mosques, religious schools and community facilities across the world from Columbus, Ohio to Cambodia are refreshed with Saudi funds.

Meanwhile, Salafism, a kind of 'Wahhabism Lite', has been gaining traction amongst the disaffected Muslim youth of Europe, North Africa and the Middle East. Salafism offers both a way of life, based on a return to the (idealised) piety of 7th-century Islam, and a political philosophy in which the West, and Western-style governments generally, are seen as obstacles to the establishment of a global Caliphate. At once traditional and modern, Salafism is agile in its exploitation of political events, using mobile phones, websites and social media to spread its message. Since the beginning of the Arab revolts of 2011, Saudi Arabia has been financing Salafist parties in Tunisia, Egypt, and even as far afield as Indonesia, with a view to undermining or obstructing democratic developments.

Wahhabi leaders have long ceased to advocate violent revolt within their homeland, where they are more interested in preserving the power of the al-Saud dynasty. However, plenty of Saudis sympathise with violent Islamist groups. This has led to a schizophrenic situation in which the government in Riyadh attempts to combat al-Qaida and Islamic State, while rich Saudis (often themselves holding high office in government) finance the radicals. Many Arabs in the Gulf region and elsewhere see in such groups new versions of the Prophet and his cohorts, who first sought to bring purity and justice to the corrupt city-states of 7th-century Arabia.

'Arab Afghans' and 'The Base Register'

Back to Afghanistan in the 1980s. The Saudi alliance and the jihad against the Soviet occupiers was, from the American point of view, a triumph – all the more so because the costs of the war were largely shouldered by Riyadh. What the Americans had not foreseen, however, was how the success of this 'holy war' would inspire other radical Islamists all over the world to declare their own jihads against oppressive regimes – or against 'the West' as a whole.

The mujahideen who passed through Pakistan to Afghanistan from all over the Islamic world were of little military significance other than as cannon fodder (though their suicide bombings and attacks helped demoralise the Soviet soldiers). However, many fought in the belief that that, having defeated a world power in the name of Islam, they would raise a new

Caliphate, the first ever on the Hindu Kush. Other Arabs, eager to be in at the start of the new world order, moved to adjacent Pakistan with their families; at the start of the 1990s the Arab communities there totalled about 30,000. In return for its co-operation, the Pakistani government received billions of dollars from Washington and Riyadh, though it kept itself out of the proxy war across the border.

Osama bin Laden was quick to capitalise on the reserve army of support in Pakistan. Newly-arrived mujahideen frequently lacked contacts on the ground; without a network, supplies or training, their passage into the ranks of the rebels frequently depended on luck. In 1982, bin Laden set up a 'Services Bureau' in the Pakistani border town of Peshawar, to recruit Arabs and despatch them safely to the battle zones. This, along with the 'House of the Supporters', essentially a hostel for bachelor jihadis set up in the town two years later, put in place a system for conveying eager young men towards the fight. Four years later, using a mixture of private wealth and CIA funds, bin Laden set up his own training camps within Afghanistan itself. These were supplied with weapons and even rudimentary training by the Americans, with the US General Consulate in Peshawar serving as much as a logistics hub as a diplomatic mission.

The 'Arab Afghans' came and went. Some stayed only briefly; others made jihad their life's mission. Bin Laden began to compile a directory of 'fighting Arab brothers', recording the CVs and military know-how of the volunteers. Before long the register had grown so large that he and his followers felt the need for a name to help them publicise their project. They settled on 'the Base Register', abbreviated to just 'the Base' – *al-Qaida* in Arabic. In other words, the terror group whose actions changed the world on 11 September 2001 was named after a database.

Moscow began to withdraw its troops from Afghanistan in 1988, but by that time Osama bin Laden had already decided to take jihad to the Arabic world. His aim was to bring down all pro-Western governments – starting with his homeland, Saudi Arabia. At the start of the first Gulf War in 1990, American (hence infidel) troops were stationed on the same soil as the holy cities of Mecca and Medina; they remained even after the end of the conflict. No doubt, wounded vanity was another factor in bin-Laden's hatred of the al-Sauds. He had approached Riyadh with the suggestion that his mujahideen could be used as a liberating force after Saddam invastion of Kuwait, but had been snubbed in favour of the Americans. As time went on, many moderate Arabs came to share bin Laden's horror at the presence of infidel boots on sacred Saudi soil. From 1998, the Americans started to shift their headquarters to the neighbouring Emirate of Qatar, but it wasn't until 2003 that the last bases in Saudi Arabia were closed.

Bin Laden soon came to the attention of the Saudi and American secret services, and was forced to flee from Saudi Arabia via Sudan back to Afghanistan. There, from the mid-1990s onwards, he planned and organised several spectacular attacks, among them 9/11. All the while, the database gave him invaluable access to fighters and allies across the Arab world.

After the Soviet withdrawal from Afghanistan, the Moscow-loyal government had held onto power for three years, until the mujahideen finally conquered Kabul. They were hopelessly divided among themselves, though, and the Islamic state they declared was little more than a cobbling-together of local and regional leaders on the hunt for booty. The Pakistani secret service, ISI, had several Afghan warlords on their payroll at this time – most notably the man known as 'the Butcher of Kabul', Gulbaddin Hekmatyar. His supporters fired on the hitherto undamaged capital with mortar shells and rockets, reduced large parts of the city to ashes, and claimed around 50,000 lives.

Afghanistan descended into anarchy, split along ethnic and religious fault-lines, until in 1994 a new movement emerged, promising security and order. From the city of Kandahar in the south, the Taliban began its triumphal march over the rubble of the mujahideen tyranny. Within two years, they had conquered Kabul.

The Taliban also cooperated closely with the ISI, and recruited almost exclusively from Pashtuns, the majority ethnic group in Afghanistan and parts of Pakistan. Their strongholds were Pakistan's numerous religious high schools, the *madrassas*. These had proliferated under the rule of the dictator General Zia ul-Haq, who seized power in a coup in 1977 and ruled until 1988. To consolidate his grip on the country, ul-Haq had promoted Islamicisation, and funded hundreds of madrassas, into whose care Pakistan's destitute families happily delivered their sons. These religious students – the word for them is *Taliban* in Pashto – were joined by many thousands of child refugees from the Afghan conflict, being fed and housed (in a co-finance deal between Pakistan and the CIA) and also being indoctrinated in Wahhabism. The lines between religious boarding schools, weapons depots and jihadi recruitment centres swiftly became blurred. And, though the *madrassas* remained at the heart of the movement, many a veteran of the war against the Soviets discerned the way the wind was blowing and joined the Taliban too.

A Sordid Affair

At the start of the US offensive on 7 October 2001, the Taliban controlled approximately 90 percent of Afghanistan, the only exception being the non-Pashtun areas in the north, where most inhabitants – the Tadjiks, Uzbeks and Hazara – are of Turkic ethnicity and Shiite belief. Initially the Taliban had no particular anti-American or anti-Western orientation, and visitors from the West could move freely and safely with Taliban-controlled parts of the country. All that changed within a fortnight, in August 1998. On 7 August – the eighth anniversary of American troops' arrival on Saudi soil – al-Qaida cells activated simultaneous truck bomb explosions outside the US embassies in Nairobi, Kenya and Dar Es Salaam, Tanzania, claiming 224 lives, wounding thousands, and providing, for many people around the world, the first introduction to bin Laden and his organisation. Thirteen days later, American cruise missiles retaliated by destroying bin Laden's training camps in Afghanistan.

Up to this point, the US government had been on notably good terms with the Taliban. The group's representatives had paid frequent visits to Washington to negotiate the construction of a natural gas pipeline from Uzbekistan to Pakistan via Afghanistan, in which the US energy concern Halliburton showed a leading interest. There were even discussions about handing over bin Laden, either to the Saudis or to the US. But the cruise missile attack put paid to all that.

From August 1998 on, the Taliban categorically refused to hand over their 'honoured guest', and adopted the hostile stance towards the US that endures to the present. (Of course it may well be that they couldn't have handed bin Laden over even if they'd wanted to: his money, his network of contacts and his aura as a 'faith warrior' helped him to stay hidden.) In response, Washington set up an economic embargo against Afghanistan, which came into force in November 1999. With this, the battle lines were finally drawn, and Osama bin Laden was able to make his preparations for 9/11 undisturbed.

Among many ironies, perhaps the most sickening is that the path to today's global war on terror began in domestic farce. Three days before the missile attacks on Afghanistan, US President Clinton had confessed on national television to an inappropriate relationship with a young White House intern, Monica Lewinsky. Much of the previous year had seen Clinton unable to act on domestic policy due to the scandal. Many commentators saw the assault on Afghanistan as a diversion or a show of strength from a domestically-weakened leader. Just over three years later, they had cause to wonder whether the lives of 3,000 Americans – and hundreds of thousands of Iraqi and Afghan civilians – might have been spared had the President only left the work-experience girl alone.

'MISSION ACCOMPLISHED': AMERICA SETS THE SCENE FOR ISLAMIC STATE

From the 1953 coup to the Afghan jihad, the same pattern can be discerned: a string of short-lived American triumphs sets the scene for future disaster, the collapse of states, and the triumph of extremism. This cycle is by no means over. It continues into the present, in ever new configurations of catastrophe. The guiding principle behind Washington's actions is hard to miss: tolerate no power in the region that is not a fully paid-up champion of Western interests. Hence the fixation with Iran, which leads us to the next chapter of our never-ending story: the Iraq-Iran war between 1980 and 1988.

Saddam Hussein was a criminal despot who, like not a few other criminal despots, owed his position to the support he had received from the West. Hussein, a trained army officer, seized power in 1979. Perhaps falling for his own propaganda, he soon came to view post-Shah Iran as easy (and rich) pickings. The Shatt al-Arab had been a disputed border zone between the two countries since the 17th century, while the Iranian province of Kuzistan contained not only a majority Arab population, but a great quantity of oil refineries. Faced with a volatile, revolutionary Islamic Republic in the heart of the Middle East, many Western and Arab powers saw Saddam as the right horse to back.

The war began in September 1980. In its first few months, the Iraqi army advanced far into Iranian territory. In mid-1982, however, came the counter attack, conducted with the help of 'human waves', thousands of religiously-inspired children and teenagers, each one sent across the mine fields with a plastic key around his neck to open the gates of heaven. These flesh-and-blood minesweepers cleared the way for the Iranian soldiers, also brimming with religious zeal. Saddam's army found itself in serious trouble and would have lost the war had the Americans not intervened on their side, prolonging hostilities for a further six years. On 20 December 1983, a photograph was taken as Donald Rumsfeld, then President Reagan's special envoy, shook hands with Saddam Hussein in Baghdad, guaranteeing US support in the form of arms and money, and confirming Washington's desire to prevent an Iranian victory at any cost. Twenty years later, that photograph would be an embarrassment to US Secretary of Defence Rumsfeld as he tried to topple Saddam, and a potent symbol of America's pernicious foreign policy.

'Everything We Can To Prevent Baghdad's Defeat'

Prolonging the war turned out to be very expensive. Iraq received massive financial support from the Gulf States, above all from Saudi Arabia, and billions in loans from Washington – though these, since the Iraqis were now obliged to import their wheat from the US, had the effect of boosting the American economy. Iraq's ballooning government debt laid the foundation stone for the region's next disaster: the invasion of Kuwait in 1990.

The US government had known since 1983 that Saddam Hussein had used poison gas both against Iranian troops and against Kurdish rebels in his own country. After some hesitation, the Reagan government publicly condemned this use of chemical weapons and half-heartedly sought to curb their export. Meanwhile, Iran made repeated attempts to get the United Nations to outlaw their use, and Washington (mindful that there were jobs at stake in the US, as well as Germany and France) repeatedly blocked them.

In January 1995, in the wake of the Iran-Contra affair, former National Security Council Director Howard Teicher made the following affidavit before a court in Florida:

> In June, 1982... President Reagan decided that the United States would do whatever was necessary and legal to prevent Iraq from losing the war with Iran. President Reagan formalized this policy by issuing a National Security Decision Directive ('NSDD') to this effect... CIA Director Casey personally spearheaded the effort to ensure that Iraq had sufficient military weapons, ammunition and vehicles to avoid losing the Iran-Iraq war... The United States actively supported the Iraqi war effort by supplying the Iraqis with billions of dollars of credits, by providing US military intelligence and advice to the Iraqis, and by closely monitoring third-country arms sales to Iraq to make sure that Iraq had the military weaponry required.[5]

Yet, as Teicher went on to testify, the US was at the same time delivering weapons to Iran. The Shah had been the largest foreign purchaser of US military hardware. Now, the stock he'd bought was becoming obsolete and outdated, and the Ayatollah's regime needed fresh supplies. They obtained these via middle men and on the black market, in Europe, Asia and South America. Evidently this trade fired the imagination of the secret services, since the CIA eventually set up a triangular operation to sell weaponry to

---

5 Sworn Court Declaration of Howard Teicher, United States District Court, Southern District of Florida, 31 January 1995. (http://www.informationclearinghouse.info/article1413.htm)

Iran, via third parties that included Israel. In a further refinement of capitalist spy-craft, the proceeds of these sales were used to finance the right-wing Contra rebels, who were attempting to topple the socialist Sandinista government in Nicaragua.

To this day it remains unclear whether this complex operation was sanctioned at the highest level. During the congressional hearings in 1987, President Reagan was unable to recall anything about it, and William J. Casey, the former CIA boss, had just died. There was public outrage, certainly, though less over the triangular trading itself than over the surrounding circumstances. The official story was that at least part of the funds was earmarked for paying ransoms to free Americans held hostage in Lebanon, but this was not the case. It also became known that the Contras had been smuggling tons of cocaine into the US for years, with the full knowledge and approval of the CIA.

In 1988, the Iraq-Iran war ended with a truce. The old borders were unchanged. A million people had lost their lives in the conflict, three-quarters of them Iranian. In 1979 Iraq had over $35 billion of gold reserves; after the war the country was indebted to the tune of $80 billion. At the same time, the price of a barrel of oil fell to ten dollars, mainly due to overproduction on the part of Kuwait and the United Arab Emirates. Indeed, Kuwait was far exceeding the agreed extraction quotas at the Rumaila oil field, which, since it spanned the border, was shared with Iraq. Saddam Hussein's regime could see no way to shed its own huge burden of debt, and neither the Gulf States nor the US were prepared to offer meaningful concessions. Saddam had already threatened war with Kuwait in the past, following border skirmishes around Rumaila, so it was not entirely surprising that, in the first months of 1990, he and his closest circle made the fateful decision to invade. On 2 August of that year, Iraq occupied Kuwait, becoming, at a stroke, the largest oil-producing country on the planet.

The Iraqi dictator knew very well that American policy vis-à-vis the Gulf States was determined by the Carter Doctrine of 1980, according to which the US would, if necessary, use force to protect its 'national interests'. Kuwait at the time was, alongside Saudi Arabia, the largest supplier of oil to the Americans. Conflict might therefore have seemed inevitable. However, just a week before the invasion, April Glaspie, the US Ambassador to Iraq, had told Saddam: 'We know you need funds. We understand that, and our opinion is that you should have the opportunity to rebuild your country [...] We have no opinion on your Arab–Arab conflicts, such as your dispute with Kuwait.'[6]

Saddam understood these diplomatic phrases as a veiled approval of the imminent attack. After all, Washington was well aware that 30,000 Iraqi soldiers had amassed on the border with Kuwait; the US fleet in the Persian Gulf was already on alert. Had the US ambassador thumped the table with her fist and warned him in no uncertain terms of the consequences of his actions, perhaps the course of history would have been different.

The Gas Station is Liberated...

The Americans assembled an international coalition under their leadership, and on 17 January 1991 the military operation to liberate Kuwait was launched. Six weeks later, the Iraqis had been driven out, although as they retreated they had set the oil fields on fire. Meanwhile, within Iraq, the Shiites in

---

6 Global Research Centre For Research On Globalization: Transcript of Meeting Between Iraqi President, Saddam Hussein and U.S. Ambassador to Iraq, April Glaspie. – July 25, 1990 (www.globalresearch.ca)

the south rose up against the ruling Sunnis, assuming that the Americans would come to their aid. This was a miscalculation. The Bush government wanted at all costs to avoid becoming embroiled in Iraqi internal affairs. At least, that particular Bush government did. In 2003, of course, George W. Bush would take a different path.

The Kuwait war illustrates the malign chain of cause and effect that often issues from an ill-conceived original act. Washington had wanted to see Iran weakened at any price during the Iraq-Iran conflict, and had intervened to achieve this. Yet the result was looming Iraqi bankruptcy – which in turn gave rise to the next war, when Saddam Hussein, still notionally a Cold War ally of the West, fell out of favour after attacking America's gas station. The liberation of Kuwait cost about $62 billion, half of which was paid by Saudi Arabia, with Britain, Germany and other European nations also footing a share of the bill. On the quiet, the Americans may even have made a profit.

After the invasion of Kuwait, the familiar pattern asserted itself. With lightning speed Saddam Hussein mutated in Western media and political discourse into the very personification of irrationality, fanaticism and cruelty. Now, for the first time, he was rebuked for the 1988 poison gas attack on the Kurdish town of Halabja, which killed as many as 5,000 people (by and large the Western businesses who had supplied the weapons escaped censure, and were seldom even mentioned). Saddam's brutal suppression of the Shiite uprising sparked the predictable comparisons with Hitler.

Of greater consequence, however, was UN Security Council Resolution 661, which on the initiative of the Americans was passed on 6 August 1990, and would eventually be lifted only after the fall of Saddam in 2003. It imposed a comprehensive economic embargo against Iraq, from which only 'supplies intended strictly for medical purposes, and, in humanitarian circumstances, foodstuffs' were excluded, and only provided these were approved by the sanctions committee.

That approval proved very hard to come by. The US and Britain set the tone, deploying sanctions deliberately to engineer hunger, poverty and hardship, and thus trigger a popular revolt against the Saddam regime. In practice, this strategy became an instrument of mass murder. The committee allowed hardly any medicines, medical equipment or important chemicals into Iraq, even outlawing the import of chlorine for the purification of drinking water. Not even pencils could be brought into the country, the reason generally cited for their ban being their potential for 'dual use' i.e. for use by the army.

In 1999, shortly before Christmas, the British government blocked the export of vaccinations against diphtheria and yellow fever for Iraqi children, arguing that they could 'be used in weapons of mass destruction'. Ten years into sanctions, scarcely a single piece of medical equipment in Iraq was functional, owing to a lack of replacement parts. Even aspirin was only available, if at all, on the black market, and at monstrous prices. Sanitary towels and plasters were scarcity goods. A cancer diagnosis became a death sentence; the same went for diabetes. Anyone who couldn't afford to travel to Jordan for treatment died. Largely unnoticed by the public in the West, more than a million Iraqis lost their lives as a result of the sanctions, at least half of them children.

In March 2000, Dr Jawad Al-Ali, a cancer specialist and member of Britain's Royal College of Physicians spoke to the *Guardian* about the dust contaminating the air in and around Basra.

It carries death. Our own studies indicate that more than 40 per cent of the population in this area will get cancer: in five years' time to begin with, then long afterwards. Most of my own family now have cancer, and we have no history of the disease. It has spread to the medical staff of this hospital. We don't know the precise source of the contamination, because we are not allowed to get the equipment to conduct a proper scientific survey, or even to test the excess level of radiation in our bodies. We suspect depleted uranium, which was used by the Americans and British in the Gulf War right across the southern battlefields.[7]

Meanwhile the Sanctions Committee continued to hinder delivery of vital equipment, including chemotherapy drugs and painkillers, and American and British planes were carrying out almost daily attacks, killing thousands of civilians whose deaths were written off under that careful term, *collateral damage*. In 1998, Denis Halliday, Assistant Secretary-General at the UN and one of the 'Humanitarian Coordinators' in Iraq, resigned from his office in protest: 'The policy of economic sanctions is totally corrupt. We are in the process of destroying an entire society. It is as simple and terrifying as that [...] Five or six thousand children are dying every month.'[8]

Children Dying: 'A price worth paying'

The Iraqi people did not hold Saddam responsible for their suf-

---

7 'Squeezed to death', John Pilger, *Guardian* 4 March 2000.

8 'UN aid chief resigns over Iraq sanctions', Patrick Cockburn, *Independent*. 30 September, 1998

fering. They blamed the West. The sanctions annihilated the previously robust middle classes, creating sky-rocketing inflation and driving them into poverty. Soon only a tiny group of wealthy people surrounding to the regime were left. The remaining 90–95% of the population lived from hand to mouth. Only in the Kurdish north was the situation less dramatic. With Western support, including an enforced no-fly-zone for Iraqi fighter jets, the region began its journey towards autonomy and *de facto* independence.

In Baghdad around this time it was common to meet taxi drivers in tattered Armani or Boss designer suits, former university lecturers or ex-CEOs, for whom holidays in Switzerland had once been nothing special, but who now struggled to feed their families. In 1989 the literacy rate of Iraq had been 95%, the highest in the Arab world; by 2000 it had fallen by more than half. The health service, formerly one of the best in the world, was in ruins. Within ten years, the incidence of child mortality had gone from one of the lowest in the world to among the highest. The systematic impoverishment of the Iraqi people, directly brought about by the US and Great Britain, is one of the least-known, or rather the least-acknowledged, crimes committed by the West since World War II. It is a prime cause, not only of the fall of the Iraqi government, but of the collapse of civil society and civilized values. A few years and another war later, this collapse would pave the way for a reign of terror under Islamic State and assorted other paramilitary groups.

On 12 May 1996, the host of the popular American TV news show '60 Minutes' put a question to Secretary of State Madeleine Albright: 'We have heard that about half a million children have died. I mean that's more children than died in Hiroshima. Is the price worth it?' This was Madeleine Albright's answer: 'I think this is a very hard choice, but the price – we think the price is worth it.' Almost two years later, in February 1998, CNN filmed Albright addressing a rowdy audience in Columbus, Ohio. 'I am willing to make a bet to anyone here,' she said, 'that we care more about the Iraqi people than Saddam Hussein does... If we have to use force, it is because we are America. We are the indispensable nation. We stand tall and we see further than other countries into the future, and we see the danger here to all of us.'

It might seem self-evident that the liberation of Kuwait in February 1991 would remove the foundation for UN Resolution 661, and with it the legal justification for sanctions. The American Empire doesn't work like that, though. Just before the Kuwait war, President George Bush Senior declared, perfectly in line with the Carter Doctrine of 1980:

> 'Access to oil in the Persian Gulf and the security of our friends in the region are vital to preserve national security in the USA (...) The United States are determined to defend their fundamental interests in the region, with military force if need be, from any power whose interests may damage our own.'[9]

Saddam's lunge for the Kuwait oil fields meant put him behond the pale. His insolence demanded retribution, regardless of the human consequences. And that retribution was meant to send a warning to the other leaders in the region: don't mess with us.

Shortly after his inauguration in 1993, President Clinton announced a new foreign policy doctrine: 'Dual Containment'. Referring to both Iraq and Iran, this marked the beginning of

---

9 National Security Directive 54, 15 January, 1991.

a more confrontational approach, and one that effectively ruled out the possibility of a fresh start in US relations with Iran. Instead, economic sanctions were now imposed on the Islamic Republic as well as Saddam's Iraq, also with the aim of weakening the government and bringing about regime change. The UN Security Council, with Britain and the US taking the lead, adopted 13 follow-up resolutions to 661, right up until Saddam's fall from power, all meant to widen the scope of the existing sanctions. Always in the background was the allegation that Iraq was developing biological and chemical weapons, circumventing the Treaty on the Non-Proliferation of Nuclear Weapons, and pursuing 'Weapons of Mass Destruction'. Yet years of UN-led inspections could not substantiate these claims. The 'smoking gun' was never found.

Toppling Saddam

Nevertheless, in 1998 the neo-conservative thinktank 'Project for the New American Century' wrote an open letter to President Clinton demanding that Saddam's regime be overthrown in order to prevent it acquiring 'Weapons of Mass Destruction'. The letter was signed by the *crème de la crème* of American neo-conservatives, including lawyer and diplomat John R. Bolton, political advisor and former assistant Secretary of Defence Richard Perle, former Defence Secretary Donald Rumsfeld, and the former World Bank President, Paul Wolfowitz.

What is neo-conservatism? In a nutshell, a messianic belief in a global *Pax Americana*. For neo-cons, values – freedom, democracy, the rule of law – are weapons used to further the cause of worldwide American hegemony. Economically, the order of the day is untrammelled financial capitalism. To put it a different way: neo-conservatism equals a social-Darwinist belief that 'might is right' mixed with megalomania and cynicism.

With the election of George W. Bush in 2000, neo-conservatism came to power. The new president placed the above-mentioned signatories in powerful positions and, shortly after his inauguration, the National Security Council broached the topic of regime change in Iraq for the first time. Six months later, in July 2001, the Ministry of Defence laid concrete plans for a military intervention which Saddam's old friend, Donald Rumsfeld, promised would give the US 'a much-improved position in the region *and elsewhere.*'[10]

The only question was: how could such a clear breach of international law be justified? There is no need to buy into conspiracy theories to see that the terrorist attacks of 11 September 2001 proved very helpful to America's pre-existing foreign policy objectives. The cabinet discussed this the very day after 9/11 – conveniently ignoring the fact that Baghdad had nothing whatever to do with the attack. While there was general agreement that an immediate 'War on Terror' should be launched, there were differences in opinion about the order of events. First Afghanistan then Iraq? Or the other way around? Nervous of public opinion, Secretary of State Colin Powell recommended focusing first on al-Qaida and then Iraq. In the case of Afghanistan, the US sought and received a UN mandate. In the case of Iraq, Washington was dependent on a 'coalition of the willing' led by the US and Britain. Russia, China and France, all permanent members of the UN Security Council with the power of veto, were against.

The reasons the US gave for invading Iraq varied in everything but their basic lack of honesty. Sometimes they argued that

---

10 Communication from Donald Rumsfeld to Condoleezza Rice, 27 July 2001, unclassified January 2009, (http://papers.rumsfeld.com/about)

getting rid of Saddam was necessary for the democratization of the Middle East. Sometimes they accused the Iraqi government of contacting 9/11 terrorist Mohammad Atta via its embassy in Prague. Above all, they claimed repeatedly that Iraq possessed 'Weapons of Mass Destruction'. The high point of these machinations – and a low point in American integrity – was Colin Powell's speech before the UN Security Council on 5 February 2003, when the Secretary of State presented allegedly indisputable evidence that Saddam Hussein did indeed hold biological and chemical 'Weapons of Mass Destruction.' It turned out later that this 'evidence' was a clumsy fabrication by the intelligence agencies.

Mission Accomplished!

The rest is history. On 19 March 2003 the US-led assault on Iraq began. On 7 April American and British soldiers marched into Baghdad. A week later the Pentagon declared an end to the fighting. Finally, on 1 May, President Bush gave his famous 'Mission Accomplished' speech, appropriately clad in fighter-pilot uniform, on the aircraft carrier USS Lincoln. The message was that Iraq was done and dusted. We won. End of story.

In fact, this was when things really kicked off. The Americans, fixated with toppling Saddam, had made no plans as to what would happen next. Ignorant of the history, religion or culture of the country they had conquered, they expected to be welcomed as heroic liberators. Germany and Japan after World War II were the templates. It had been possible to successfully implant democracy there, so why not in Iraq? There was hardly a neo-con who did not push this bogus comparison.

If these messianic dreamers had consulted the history books,

they would have learnt that Iraq had been artificially construct-
ed by the colonial powers after World War I. It had never been
home to a single, homogenous people who identified themselves
as 'Iraqi'. In fact, the population is comprised of three main
groups. The Sunni Kurds in the north make up around 20 percent of the total population; they are not Arabs, but are similarly divided into tribal societies and clans. Arab Sunnis in central
Iraq are similar in number; they have formed the country's ruling
elite since the early days of Ottoman rule in the 16th century.
The remaining 60 percent or so are Arab Shiites, who live mostly
in the south of the country. Iraqi oil is situated almost exclusively
in the Kurdish and the Shiite regions: the centre of the country,
home to the Sunnis, has little or none. There are several other religious and ethnic groups, including Christians and Yezidis, but
these are small in number and politically unimportant.

Saddam Hussein, from a Sunni clan in the central Tikrit region, came to power with the support of the military and the
secret service. He'd joined the pan-Arab, left-leaning Baath Party
(*Baath* means rebirth) in the late 1950s, and under his rule party
membership swiftly became a prerequisite for those wishing to
join the political elite. This Sunni elite were quick to terrorise
and exploit the Kurds and Shiites to the north and south. Within the Sunnis, however, was a further hierarchy, with all leading
positions being filled by members of Saddam's own clan, the
al-Tikriti.

The above sketch is a simplification, but it shows the sheer
wrong-headedness of the notion that Iraq could be transformed
into a US-style democracy overnight. It was this, however, that
the conquering heroes attempted to do, starting not long after
Saddam was found cowering in a hole in his tribal homelands.
The evil dictator may have been ousted, but the brave new

Saddam-free Iraq proved to be above all a dangerous arena in which the US could make a series of fatal errors.

The power vacuum that formed shortly after the invasion of Baghdad accelerated the spread of anarchy and chaos. Under the eyes of the American and British troops, all ministries (except the Ministry of Oil, which was secured by soldiers) all banks, all museums, and many other public buildings were looted. The occupiers showed little interest in providing security for the general population. They neglected to restore severely damaged water and electricity supplies. In May 2003, Paul Bremer was appointed by Bush as Presidential Envoy to Iraq. Over the next two years, in this ever fractured but now shattered country, more than half of whose population lived below the poverty line, Bremer pursued a radical neo-liberal agenda of privatisation, until the last functioning remnants of the state had been all but extinguished.

Bremer reversed the 1972 nationalisation of Iraq's oil industry, granting the new exploration rights mostly to – surprise! – US and British companies: Exxon, Chevron, Halliburton, BP and Shell. In a more than usually critical report titled 'Iraq – Ten Years On', CNN explored in 2013 the role of 'Big Oil' in George W. Bush's election campaign (to whose coffers it vastly contributed) and, later, in his administration. As expected, Bush appointed as his Vice President energy- and oil-lobbyist Dick Cheney; it was under Cheney's leadership that the newly created 'National Energy Policy Development Group' drew up plans for the redistribution of Iraqi oil among Western oil multinationals. CNN's conclusion: 'Yes, the Iraq war was a war for oil, and it was a war with winners: Big Oil.'

The occupation forces made no attempt to bring together ethnic, religious or tribal leaders in a national dialogue about how the new Iraq should be organised. Bremer did select individual representatives from each group to serve as points of contact, but fostered disunity by labelling them 'Sunnis', 'Kurds' or 'Shiites' instead of promoting a shared sense of *Iraqi* identity. His preferred advisers were dubious exiles, people with no backing or credibility within Iraq itself, but who for years had been telling the neo-conservatives what they wanted to hear. Bremer's emphasis on Iraq's sectarian and tribal divisions helped to deepen pre-existing fault-lines. There had always been linguistic, regional, tribal and religious differences, but under Saddam's secular, iron-fist of a state, they had been kept in check. Religious differences, in particular, had been of little significance, with Sunni and Shiite living side by side in the major cities and towns. But the crude categories of the Bremer administration left the people no choice other than to follow suit: if they wanted to be listened to, they had to stress the 'Sunni', 'Kurdish' or 'Shiite' nature of their concerns. Over time, this helped to fuel the rise of sectarian Islamism, from which the savagery of the Islamic State would later emerge.

The greatest mistake of all was made by Paul Wolfowitz, Deputy Defence Secretary. It was Wolfowitz who took the decision to dissolve the Iraqi army and outlaw the Baath party as a criminal association. At a stroke hundreds of thousands of Iraqis, mostly Sunnis, lost their livelihoods, been disempowered and humiliated. For the Sunnis, who had been the elite for hundreds of years, this was an unacceptable affront. In that moment, Sunni resistance to the American occupation and to the ruling majority Shiites was born, laying the foundations for terrorism and violence. Many of Saddam's former generals and officers, as well as thousands of ex-soldiers, party officials and secret service agents, began to disappear underground.

The Illusion of Democracy

In both Afghanistan and Iraq, the Western powers were keen to hold elections as soon as possible and to establish a formally democratic government with which they could do business (and which would rubber-stamp immunity for their soldiers and mercenaries). The sense of urgency meant that the systematic and flagrant electoral rigging in Afghanistan was simply ignored. Nor were the occupiers willing to face the evident truth that a nation whose state had collapsed, and whose society was both feudal in structure and riven by ethnic and religious tensions, did not offer fertile ground for democracy – least of all one that would prove little more than an instrument of outside interests.

A democracy needs stable foundations and good leadership. It needs a degree of social consensus: about the importance of checks and balances, the separation of powers, the rule of law, pluralism. Endemic poverty and violence, a society atomised by decades of dictatorship followed by an invasion and occupation in which thousands of civilian lives were lost to drone-inflicted 'collateral damage': such conditions are not conducive to peaceful, Western-style democracy. What they are conducive to is the the rise of regional warlords and the reinforcement of existing feudal structures. The role of the local politician in this scenario is depressingly familiar: notionally a leader – of a clan, a tribe, a religious or ethnic group – but in fact a mere client of foreign powers.

Nuri al-Maliki, Prime Minister of Iraq from April 2006 to August 2014, is a good example. In the first free elections in 2005, Shiite parties won the vote – not surprisingly, since Shiites make up the majority of the population. Yet the victors did not embark upon a program of equitable power-sharing or consensus-building. Instead, their program was one of long-desired vengeance. In recompense for centuries of Sunni violence – most recently the massacre in 1991 of tens of thousands of Shiites by Saddam's Republic Guard – Maliki methodically removed Sunnis from leadership positions and administrative roles, largely excluded them from any share in national resources, and in so doing swiftly fanned the flames of a Sunni uprising.

From 2010, during his second term, Maliki served not just as Prime Minister but also as Home and Defence secretaries, head of the Secret Service and Commander-in-chief of the Army. He used death squads to snuff out Sunni protests, and frequently levelled half-baked accusations of terrorism at his Sunni deputy. Yet for years he enjoyed the support both of Washington and Tehran. One ironic by-product of the invasion was to create an alliance between Iran and Shiite-ruled Iraq. The more power the Shiites wielded – and the more brutally they wielded it – the more Sunnis were driven into the arms of jihadi extremists like Islamic State. Amidst rising violence and polarization, it became all but impossible for Iraqis of differing confessions or ethnicities to unite against the mounting threat.

Sunnis versus Shiites

Iraq, successively traumatised by sanctions, state collapse, and the impotence of its new government, became a breeding ground for militias and terrorist organisations, both Sunni and Shiite. The uprising against the American occupation (2003–2011) was carried out mostly by Sunnis, under the direction of Islamists. Al-Qaida established itself in Iraq under the leadership of the barely-literate Jordanian Bedouin, Abu Musab al-Zarkawi. After he was killed by an American bomb in 2006, a new group

47

emerged from al-Qaida in Iraq. At first it called itself 'Islamic State of Iraq', then 'Islamic State of Iraq and the Levant'. Since June 2014 it has been known as 'Islamic State'.

Radical Sunnis didn't fight only the Americans and their allies. They also bombed markets and busy town squares in Shiite districts. Shiites responded in kind, and Baghdad became a divided city. It became highly dangerous for a Sunni to visit a Shiite part of the city, and vice-versa. Thousands fled. Ten years after the invasion, the Sunni proportion of the capital's total population had shrunk from almost half to about 20 percent. With Iran backing the Shiites and Saudi Arabia supporting the Sunnis, the internal Iraqi conflict became a confessionally-charged proxy war, claiming up to 3,000 lives a month. Religion was not the cause, but a fault-line that could be exploited in a conflict that was really about power and resources. The Americans and their allies reacted in their usual manner: with more soldiers and more money to buy the support of more – equally ambivalent – tribal leaders. This did as little to calm the situation as the occupiers' continuing brutality, a mere glimpse of which was broadcast to the world in the infamous Abu Ghraib photographs.

The number of deaths in Iraq during the invasion and its aftermath is disputed: estimates vary drastically and there are no official statistics. Between 30,000 and 150,000 lives (including both soldiers and civilians) were lost up to the point when US troops occupied Baghdad. Since then, at least half a million people have been killed, whether through resisting the occupation or in internal conflicts among Iraqis. It seems safe to assume that at least two million Iraqis have lost their lives since the Kuwait invasion of 1990, whether as a result of violence or of sanctions. The death toll is still rising, as the bloody conflict in Syria continues to spill over into the surrounding regions.

'GOOD' AND 'BAD' JIHADIS: HOW THE WEST FAILS TO LEARN FROM ITS MISTAKES

Iraq is just one of many countries in the region where the situation is dramatic. Storms are brewing all over the Arab world. Entire states have collapsed under the influence of murderous, Islamist militias (as in Libya, Syria and Yemen, and partially in Lebanon and Sudan), or they have stiffened into the deceptive calm of autocracy (as in Egypt and the Gulf States). Little remains of the hopes for freedom and democracy promised by the Arab Spring only a few years ago. The mood is of resignation and fatalism. Western observers tend to lay the blame at the foot of religion (Islam = Dark Ages, barbarism, etc.), but this misconstrues the real causes. Across an area from Algeria to the Gulf, Syria to Sudan, tribal, local and regional forces disrupt progress, while deep-rooted poverty, lack of education, and patriarchal structures all favour the status quo rather than revolution. The desire for a better life cannot in itself effect change.

Even so, the Arab world has been shedding its skin, and the contours of a new order are slowly becoming apparent, thought it is a long way from taking on a meaningful political form. There is a fundamental tension between the 'old' Arab world (rural, tribal, traditional, feudal, with hierarchical authority running right through family, society and state) and the 'new' (urban, individual, global, forward-looking). The Gulf States, such as Abu Dhabi and Dubai, express the conflict perfectly: sci-fi city-skylines, money the only limit on possibility, alongside an antiquated legal system that punishes rape victims for 'adultery' and flogs criminals.

The Arab Spring was an attempt on the part of the urban youth – with the help of the 'street' and the internet – to create a new political order. It was an attempt to move away from the Kings and the Generals, the tribal leaders and token democrats whose energies in the decades since independence had been devoted largely to empowering and enriching themselves and their families at the expense of their countries. For such leaders, the state and its resources often seemed little more than their own private property.

The revolts of 2011 swept some of these individuals aside, but it could not change the underlying structures. The social group from which the insurgents came – essentially the young, urban middle class – was simply too weak to undermine the *ancien régime*. An alliance of Islamists and secular forces, made up of both rich and poor, united by hatred of their ruler, did come together briefly on Tahrir Square in Cairo, but it was too short-lived to lead the revolt to a lasting victory.

During the French Revolution of 1789, the people seized power from the King, the clergy and the nobility. Feudalism began to give way to a modern, industrial society in a slow and bloody process that extended far into the twentieth century, and was accompanied by many backlashes, counter-revolutions and wars. In the end, though, modernisation and mechanisation won out against the *ancien régime*. Economic dynamics swept absolutism away. A successful revolution like the one in France (or for that matter in Iran in 1979) needs a solid block of social power to ensure that change does not stop with the toppling of monuments and demagogues, but that something is built to replace them. In Iran, this was an alliance between the clergy and the bazaar. In 18th- and 19th-century Europe, it was the emerging middle classes. And these middle classes were precisely what the Arab Spring lacked.

Clans, Tribes and Missing Classes

At the core of the tragic predicament of today's Arab world is its hybrid, conflicted nature, in which the medieval and the modern co-exist. No country from Morocco to Oman has urban middle classes strong enough to reshape absolutist monarchies into constitutional ones, or to replace military dictatorships with parliamentary democracies. The Egyptians may have managed to topple Mubarak – but only Mubarak. The military regime was untouched, and ready to retaliate. It has since proven itself more repressive than Mubarak ever was. Only in Iraq was there a strong middle class that might eventually have been able to de-throne Saddam – before, that is, it was pulverised by sanctions.

The Arab middle classes, nowhere more than 40 percent of the population and generally less, have shallow roots. They live with the ever-present threat of sinking back into the rural poverty from which their parents or grandparents came. Unsurprisingly, the struggle to stay afloat often takes precedence over challenging the power of the clans and tribes, or deep-rooted religious and ethnic divisions. Despite the enormous wealth of the Gulf States, the Arab world has experienced little or no industrial revolution. At its core it remains backward-looking and feudal in structure, with the oil paying for an army of foreigners to keep the economic wheels turning.

With this flaw at the heart of the Arab Spring, the outcome everywhere, with the possible exception of Tunisia (see below) was failure, albeit with local variations. In Egypt, the power vacuum left by Mubarak was filled by Field Marshall el-Sisi, a case of one dictator warming the seat for another. In the Gulf States, representatives of the old order either pumped out money to buy their subjects' loyalty, or they fell back on the tried-and-tested means of repression. In Syria, the revolt paved the way to the chaos and carnage of civil war.

Nevertheless, it is still too early to pronounce the forces of progress which found expression in the Arab Spring dead and buried. Large parts of today's Arab world are reminiscent of the Europe of the Thirty Years' War (1618–1648). It will be a very long time – decades at least, perhaps generations – before hatred and violence give way to freedom, prosperity and democracy. There may be no happy ending. The protesters wanted a better world. They got Sisi and Islamic State. It is a bitter irony.

Clan, tribe, denomination, ethnicity. These are the hallmarks of today's feudal states in the East, and all such states, old or new, use them for their own purposes. Individual identity is subsumed by the identity of the group. Western-style individualism, dependent on conditions of mobility and modernity, cannot begin to emerge in these straitened social circumstances, let alone thrive. The same goes for reformist religious ideas – ones that allow, for example, a non-literal interpretation of the Koran.

In large cities, there were signs of new social groupings and identities, but they didn't last long when violence and state collapse forced people to look to their survival. Under such pressures, they inevitably fell back on centuries-old solidarities. Woe betide the Kurd, Christian or Shiite, or even the liberal-minded Sunni, who happens across a road blockade in Syria or Iraq guarded by the Islamic State.

Denominationalism and tribalism go hand in hand with

intolerance and violence towards people belonging to other groups. Power is understood not as a means of arbitrating disputes between rival interests but of forcing others into line – or, failing that, of destroying them. This applies to secular despots like Saddam Hussein and Bashar al-Assad, as well as radical Islamists. They seek not compromise, but ultimate victory; and their opponents are no different. It is particularly important to note this point in the context of Syria. A popular perception in the West is that Bashar al-Assad is single-handedly responsible for millions of refugees, the deaths of 200,000 people and the destruction of the country. It follows, so the argument goes, that Damascus must be isolated and Assad toppled – if necessary using military force – in order to usher into power the so-called 'moderate' opposition.

Such proposals may be steeped in the language of morality but they are based on some fundamental misinterpretations. They also look very like a modern (albeit humanitarian-inflected) version of imperialism. What grounds are there to believe that democracy, freedom and the rule of law will be established once Assad is gone? What would prevent the Sunnis, who comprise 60% of the Syrian population, from simply seizing power? Would they act differently to the Shiites in post-Saddam Iraq, and refrain from meting out revenge to Assad supporters? Would democracy emerge, or just another dictatorship, no less bloody or massacre-prone than the previous one? Last but not least, which particular Sunnis would be most likely to seize power? The answer, given the balance of military power in the region, is the radical Islamists.

Proponents of interventionism, whether on humanitarian or other grounds, dispute this. They like to refer to Syrian 'civil society' – though this has been all but wiped out by the war – and cling to an unwavering belief in the 'moderate' Syrian opposition. Yet this is largely a phantom of the Western imagination. The exiled Syrians who came together to form the 'National Coalition' pay lip service to the idea of moderation, but most of their energy is taken up with fighting among themselves. What's more, they have no discernible influence in Syria itself. To understand just how woefully inadequate the Western interventionist program for Syria is, we need to zoom in a little closer on the history of the conflict.

Syria: First Sparks

Inspired by the rebellions in North Africa, the first spontaneous protests in Syria began in January and February 2011. For the most part, these were organised by small groups of inexperienced, city-based activists, and were focussed on issues like corruption or general social problems.

A month or so later, the situation escalated when security forces in Deraa, a city on the border of Jordan, imprisoned a group of young protesters who had painted the walls with anti-government graffiti. When parents tried to get their children released, the police responded with brutal violence. Images of these scenes spread across the internet and triggered protests across the whole of Syria, though they didn't reach the scale of the mass movements of Egypt or Tunisia. In Damascus and Aleppo, anti-Assad demonstrations were confined to the city outskirts, while Hama, Syria's fourth largest city, located in the centre of the country, developed into a stronghold of the protest movement.

In June government security forces retreated from Hama, but they returned a few weeks later, this time with tanks and heavy artillery. To start with the protests had been largely peaceful, but with the regime's increasingly violent response (using the secret services and the police alongside the regular army) the protesters began to arm themselves. Despite international efforts, including the involvement of former UN Secretary-General Kofi Annan, the path to civil war was cleared with the emergence of the Free Syrian Army in July. By that time, the conflict had already assumed a sectarian character.

The Alawites are generally viewed as an offshoot of Shiite Islam. They represent ten to fifteen percent of Syria's population, and have dominated the military and security services since the time of the French mandate. Curiously, it was the Alawites' traditional poverty which paved the way to their current hegemony: richer Syrians could afford to pay for their sons to be exempted from military service. It was the indentured son of one such Alawite tribe, Hafez al-Assad, who seized power in a coup in 1970, with the support of his fellow Alawites in the military.

Hafez al-Assad, who was President until his death in 2000 (whereupon his son, Bashar, a London-trained ophthalmologist, replaced him), recognised that he could not secure the hegemony of his clan by arms alone. Instead, he formed a pact with the Sunni middle classes – the traders and merchants of Damascus and Aleppo. The deal was that if they didn't question his power, he would leave them to do business unmolested. At the same time, the Baath party, the collection of Assad's cronies which nominally ruled Syria (as well as Iraq, under Saddam Hussein) worked hard to gain support for its model of a secular state, which guaranteed freedom of religion to minorities, in particular Christians and Druze, so long as they did not question the Alawites' right to rule. The minorities were happy to agree, since the only alternative – power being seized by less tolerant Sunnis in the form of the Muslim Brotherhood – was even less attractive.

The power of the Assad clan therefore rests largely on patronage (underpinned by multiple secret services). In spite of the socialist leanings of the pan-Arabist Baath Party, through whose ranks Hafez had risen and in whose name he had originally acted, this was not a dictatorship concerned with ideology, still less with the creation of a 'new human'. It was about keeping power.

During the 1970s, with grassroots support from poor Sunnis, the Syrian Muslim Brotherhood grew into an influential underground opposition movement. Its aim was the violent overthrow of the Assad regime. In 1982 the army crushed the movement, advancing on the Muslim Brotherhood's stronghold, Hama, and flattening vast parts of the city with airstrikes and artillery fire. Up to 30,000 people were killed. The message was unequivocal: all those who challenge Alawite hegemony will be destroyed. The Muslim Brotherhood has not played a role in Syria since, though they are strongly represented among the exiled opposition.

Since the first stirrings of rebellion, Hafez's son, Bashar, has played the denominational card. As early as 27 March 2011, a government spokeswoman, Bouthaina Shaaban, claimed that a prominent Qatari-based cleric had incited the wave of unrest in Syrian cities.[11] Assad himself made similar assertions, alluding to a Sunni 'conspiracy' against his regime.[12] The wheel of violence began to turn more rapidly, with Sunnis killing Alawites and vice versa. Anti-Assad activists, weak in number and fractured, could do little to stop it. Even moderate Alawite and Sunni dignitaries were unable to stem the general brutalisation and religious violence. From mid-2011, Alawite-dominated militias, loyal to the regime, began wreaking collective retribution against

11 'US Will Not Intervene In Syria As It Has In Libya, Says Hillary Clinton' *Guardian*, 27 March 2011

12 Michael Slackman, 'Syrian Leader Blames "Conspiracy" For Turmoil', *New York Times*, 30 March 2011.

Sunni villages and Sunni districts, besieging and starving the inhabitants, or simply laying waste to whole areas. Since 2012, Assad has been receiving support from Iraqi and Lebanese Shiite fighters, which has only confirmed the widespread belief among Sunnis that they are the prime target of a religiously-motivated state oppression.

At no point has Assad tried to find a path back from violence. He has followed the logic of his own clan: that compromise and concession are signs of weakness, that the goal can be nothing less than the total destruction of the enemy. His opponents, the Sunni militias, supported mainly by the US and Saudi Arabia, have followed the same logic. Hence the tragedy was free to take its blood-soaked course.

A Minority Revolt

A crucial difference between the Syrian uprising and others in the Arab World – and one that is rarely mentioned by Western politicians or opinion makers – is that neither Syria's religious minorities nor the Sunni business community have joined the opposition to Assad's regime. Since these groups make up no less than half the population, it is not surprising that the Free Syrian Army and the various radical Sunni militias have failed to conquer Damascus or Aleppo. They simply have little support there.

Until December 2016, when Assad's troops recaptured its eastern districts, Aleppo was a divided city. The west remained under the control of the regime, while the east was occupied by the insurgents, whose ranks were filled mainly from the rural areas along the border with Jordan (though few came from Hawran, where most people are Druze) and the Turkish and Iraqi border regions. Destitute Sunnis still form the backbone of the rebellion, among them many farmers and refugees who see gang life as an alternative to famine, drought and poverty. They receive a small stipend, which they are encouraged to supplement by looting and plundering. The city-dwelling, liberal-minded activists who were so vocal at the start of the rebellion are either dead, in prison, or have long since fled.

The Free Syrian Army (FSA), labelled 'moderate' by Western governments, is less an army and more a loose coalition between local and regional militias. It consists mainly of Sunni deserters from Assad's army. There is no single high command; the various leaders wage war without mutual consultation, and with predictably erratic results. It is not the hallmark of an intelligent strategy to attack an enemy where it is strongest, yet the FSA did just that by attempting to conquer Damascus and Aleppo. The result was the devastation of the city outskirts as Assad retaliated in his usual way: with bombardments and sieges of rebel-held areas. Despite this, the FSA's tactics have remained unchanged. Their fighters have as little regard for civilians as the regime. Acts of cruelty and robbery are common to both sides. When the FSA has managed to seize control of a region, it has not set up a functioning civil administration. The threat from Islamist forces, meanwhile, has often forced the FSA onto the back foot, with many of their soldiers defecting to Islamic State or other Islamist groups who, thanks to financial support from the Gulf States, were able to pay wages.

In the early days of the Syrian uprising, some experienced opponents of the regime voiced the concern that it might be premature. Perhaps they were right. In contrast to Tunisia and Egypt, Syria did not have a long history of strikes and protests. Many educated, urban activists, infected with excitement at what was happening in North Africa and blinded by wishful thinking, underestimated both the sectarian angle and Assad's determination to hold onto power. Instead of the regime change they had hoped for, the rebellion spawned a brutal civil war that set people who had been neighbours for years suddenly at each others' throats. Chaos, endemic violence and state collapse – it was only a matter of time before radical Islamist militants would step into the picture.

To make matters worse, by 2012 it had become clear that the Syrian civil conflict had turned into a proxy war between two global camps. On one side were the West, Turkey and the Gulf States, with Saudi Arabia at their head, all seeking the fall of Assad. On the other side were Russia, China and Iran, all equally determined to keep Assad in power as a way to check the influence and power of the West and its allies over the region.

Civil War Becomes Proxy War

To explain these alignments, we must look to geopolitics. The Syrian regime had always been a close ally of the Soviet Union. Partly this was due to the socialist leanings of Baath Party who seized power in 1953. More relevant, however, is the Six Day War of 1967, which ended with the Israeli occupation of the Golan Heights in Syria. Unlike the US and western European countries, Moscow backed Syria's demands for their return. The alliance between the two countries has survived the fall of the Soviet Union.

The Islamic Revolution in Iran provided a new strategic partner. After 1979, Syria became Iran's closest ally in the Arab world. When the Shiite Hezbollah party was formed in the 1980s to resist the Israeli occupation of Southern Lebanon (1982–2000), their weapons supply chain was soon passing through Damascus. The alliance between Tehran, Damascus and Hezbollah explains the long-standing efforts of the Americans and Europeans, in close cooperation with Israel, to weaken Assad's regime. In 2005, for instance, after the murder of the Lebanese Prime Minister Hariri, possibly by the Syrian Secret Services, they successfully demanded, via a UN Resolution, the withdrawal from Lebanon of all Syrian troops; these had been stationed there since the start of the civil war (1975–1990).

In February 2012, the 'Group of Friends of the Syrian People' was formed on the initiative of the French President, Nicolas Sarkozy. The idea was to bind together the West, Turkey and the Gulf States in an anti-Assad, America-led alliance whose goal was regime change. Preparations got underway: Damascus was smothered in sanctions; Assad was styled as evil personified ('butcher', 'Hitler', etc.); an opposition was built up, at first called the National Council, then the National Coalition – from their seat in Istanbul, they were meant to organise the takeover of power in Syria. Officially, of course, this was all to be done in the name of democracy and human rights, for humanitarian reasons, to end the suffering of the Syrian people... The real calculation, though, was different: with Assad gone, a Sunni regime would surely come to power, driving a wedge between Syria and Iran and turning the country towards the West. In this scenario, Hezbollah, cut off from its weapons supply, would quickly find itself with its back to the wall.

Moscow and Beijing, meanwhile, continued to support Assad as the best chance to prevent Syria falling under Western control. What happened in 2011 in Libya only toughened their stance. When the Libyan uprising broke out, both Russia and China agreed to a UN Resolution aiming to protect civilians by stopping the Gaddafi regime from launching retributory strikes against the rebel city of Benghazi in eastern Libya. However, the America-led alliance exploited this concession to pursue the quite different goal of toppling Gaddafi. It is a lesson Russia and China have not forgotten, and explains the chorus of vetoes every time the US and its allies try to push through measures against Assad's regime, or any other Resolution that might serve as a pretext for a military intervention, such as no-fly-zones or safe areas for refugees.

American and European foreign policy pays little or no heed to reconciling the interests of other large or regional powers. Instead, it stakes claim to the alleged moral high ground, and in so doing alienates all adversaries. As a result, Syria has come to a political standstill. Moscow, Tehran and Beijing are by no means immovable in their attachment to Assad, but they will only let go of him when the price is right and they see their interests safeguarded. For this to happen, the US must accept that other big hitters have joined the one-man game of the immediate post-Cold War era.

The Friends Stand Firm: Assad Must Go

On 18 July 2012 a bomb attack on the National Security Headquarters in Damascus blew apart the inner circle of power. Many leading officials were killed, including the President's brother-in-law. At this point, Assad's enemies could probably have overthrown him – if the US had been prepared to negotiate with Moscow and Tehran. At no other time has the regime been in any real danger. The majority of Syrians prefer Assad's rule to an uncertain future in which radical Islamists would hold power. The Alawites know only too well what fate they could expect if Assad were to go, and continue to support him, however much they may dislike him. As mentioned above, neither the minorities (including the Christians) nor the Sunni mercantile classes joined the opposition, and indeed some formed their own pro-government militias. The 'Friends of the Syrian People' have overlooked or deliberately ignored the fact that Syria is not Libya, that sectarian divisions create an entirely different landscape. Meanwhile, Russia and Iran kept their money on the likely eventual 'winner'.

Instead of acknowledging their mistakes and learning from them – which would admittedly have meant eating a certain amount of humble pie – the interventionists continued to intone their mantra: *Assad must go*. The two major UN Syria conferences, in June 2012 and January 2014, both ended in failure because of the West's insistence on a transitional government completely purged of Assad and his supporters. It was out of the question that Russia or Iran would agree to this, let alone Assad himself. Indeed, Iran wasn't even invited to the first Syria conference, though UN Secretary-General Ban Ki-moon tried to correct this mistake for the second – only to withdraw the invitation at the last minute due to pressure from the US.

In the interval between these two conferences, the US State Department repeatedly and publicly excoriated Russia and China. Secretary of State Hillary Clinton excelled at verbal attacks: Russia and China would 'pay dearly' for supporting Assad; they were 'obstructing' and 'abusing' the United Nations; and so on. Yet more sanctions were imposed on Damascus. The US issued regular threats of military action – but then, in August 2013, after a chemical weapons attack allegedly perpetrated by the Assad against his own people, surprised the world by abruptly cancelling the planned intervention. It was as though Obama had woken up to the difference between thundering rhetoric and an actual ground invasion with unclear fronts, the risk of international escalation, and a raft of dubious partners. Obama's decision not to send troops finally consigned the exiled opposition leaders of the 'National Coalition' to the footnotes of history; the original plan, to hand them the government of Syria after Assad fell, was summarily dropped.

The official Western version, which lays blame for the destruction of Syria solely at the feet of Assad, may have a comforting simplicity, but it falls short of the truth. The geopolitical calculations of the Friends of the Syrian People – veiled under a cloak of humanitarianism –played a decisive part. The refusal to compromise when dealing with Russia and Iran has opened the way for further state collapse and the rise of Islamic State in Syria, as has the fiction that an alternative, moderate opposition is waiting in the wings. At the same time, Syria and Iraq have become a battlefield for a dangerous proxy war between Saudi Arabia and Iran – an escalating showdown between Sunnis and Shiites, the consequences of which cannot yet be predicted.

The Dictator Changes Tack

Bashar al-Assad's regime is certainly ruthless, but it has shown remarkable pragmatism in the face of rapidly changing circumstances. For instance, it realised early that it would not be able to take back all the regions where the Sunnis had revolted. Instead, Assad's people have concentrated on bringing the core Alawite regions and the economic arteries along the line from Hawran on the Jordanian border, through Damascus and on to Aleppo, under their control. The third-largest city in the country, Homs, became the bloodiest battlefield of the war precisely because it was at the intersection of the main north-south and east-west roads. Today Homs is reminiscent of Dresden after World War II, more archaeological ruin than place of habitation. Yet the military strategy succeeded. Assad's army managed to re-conquer and consolidate power in these regions, supported massively support by Hezbollah, with their expertise in guerrilla and street fighting. Since then, the Syrian army has adopted the modus operandi of a militia group, gaining in versatility and flexibility in comparison with other combat units.

At the same time, the regime gave up on the vast, arid regions along the Turkish and Iraqi border. It concentrated mainly on fighting the Free Syrian Army, leaving the Islamist militias, foremost among them Islamic State, more or less free to do what they wished. The calculation was to allow IS to spread on both sides of the Syria-Iraq border, where it would threaten Western interests and the stability of the region (but not, crucially, Assad himself). The Kurdish regions in the north were left alone, much to the annoyance of Ankara, since the Syrian Kurds are closely allied with the outlawed Turkish Kurdish Workers' Party (PKK). Assad's response to the 'Friends of the Syrian People' was as clever as it was devastating in its consequences, preserving the Alawite regime at the cost of the stability of the entire region.

The war in Syria has metastasised far from its origins, so that it no longer makes sense to talk of a single conflict. In October 2013, the British military journal *Jane's Defence Weekly* estimated the numbers of groups, gangs, bands and militias at over 1,000. The boundary between politically-motivated violence and normal criminality such as kidnapping or robbery has become blurred out of all recognition. Outside the two biggest militias, the Nusra Front – who have close ties to al-Qaida – and Islamic State, most fighters are not ideologically motivated but simply trying to organise their own survival, often along with that of their village, clan or group. They join whoever is strongest and/or whoever pays the most. The American notion that it would be possible to take a thousand 'moderate' opposition fighters, train them and dispatch them to fight IS and Assad is laughably naïve.

Yet precisely this misguided strategy was launched on a grand scale. As early as 24 March 2013, the *New York Times* was reporting:

> with help from the CIA, Arab governments and Turkey have sharply increased their military aid to Syria's opposition fighters in recent months, expanding a secret airlift of arms and equipment for the uprising against President Bashar al-Assad (...) The airlift, which began on a small scale in early 2012 and continued intermittently through last fall, expanded into a steady and much heavier flow late last year, the data shows. It has grown to include more than 160 military cargo flights by Jordanian, Saudi and Qatari military-style cargo planes landing at Esenboga Airport near Ankara, and, to a lesser degree, at other Turkish and Jordanian airports.[13]

Who Pays the Price?

This is the classic American model, developed when fighting the Soviet occupation of Afghanistan. In those days the mujahideen were provided with weapons and intelligence by the US government; later on, these same rebels morphed into sworn enemies, in the form of the Taliban and al-Qaida. There is no guarantee that Syria's 'moderate' opposition fighters, having used

---

13 C.J. Chivers, Eric Schmidt, 'Arms Airlift To Syria Rebels Expands, With Aid From C.I.A.' *New York Times*, 24 March 2013

American dollars and expertise to topple Assad, will not join Islamic State or another Islamist group in the future. Moreover, many Muslims, even genuinely moderate ones, believe that the West is waging war on Islam itself – a notion that acts as a powerful recruiting tool for the jihadis.

It is ordinary people who pay the price. Of the 23 million inhabitants of the country, about half have fled their homes, most of them remain internally displaced within Syria. Lebanon and Turkey have taken in more than 1.5 million refugees each, Jordan around half a million. Particularly in Lebanon, these huge influxes are creating political instability and social tensions. Within Syria, centuries-old sites of cultural significance have been destroyed and the country as a whole lies devastated. An entire generation is growing up with no education or prospects.

The Syrian tragedy has the potential to unleash Armageddon because it is unfolding at a crossroads of global, power-political interests. What if the West were to launch a full-scale military intervention, not just against Islamic State but against Assad himself? Would Russia, China and Iran throw their weight further behind the regime – for example, by giving Damascus access to the top-of-the-range surface-to-air missiles Russia has until now denied?

The attempt to bring down Assad at any price, especially without a clear alternative, is lunacy. After the experiences of Iraq, Afghanistan and Libya, it should be obvious that democracy cannot be forced on a country from the outside. The Syrian uprising came at least ten years too early: the conditions necessary for a transition of power simple did not exist in 2011. This is not to absolve Assad and his regime or to downplay their crimes. But in these circumstances the following short but – among Islam thinkers – influential quote from the *Sunna*, the account of

Prophet Muhammad's life, seems especially apt: *Better sixty years of an unjust Imam than a single night without a Sultan.*

The Friends of the Syrian People might have shown themselves somewhat more deserving of their name if, instead of chasing fantasies of a moderate opposition, they had opened a dialogue with Moscow, Tehran and Beijing. It is true that these 'friends of Assad' have done nothing to persuade their ally to end the slaughter, but their indifference towards the plight of millions is only matched by that of our own representatives, who persist against all evidence in the belief that 'Western values' can sprout overnight.

Assad is pragmatic, at least where the survival of his own regime is concerned. If his supporters put enough pressure on him – which of course they won't if they have nothing to gain – he will show himself amenable to political negotiation. This would be a far better approach, especially for the people of Syria. Western powers are not notably squeamish when it comes to choosing their partners; surely it wouldn't be so hard to open a dialogue with Assad. The alternative – yet another American military intervention, the latest in a string of armed forays into the Islamic world – would be disastrous. Advocates of interventionism like to claim that IS would not have gained so much sway in the region if Assad had been removed earlier. The opposite is true. It was the Western goal of getting rid of Assad at any cost that made Islamic State so strong in the first place. If the dictator had actually fallen, these holy warriors would likely be occupying his palace in Damascus right now.

IN THE HEART OF DARKNESS:
THE SUCCESS OF 'ISLAMIC STATE'

The 'War on Terror' declared by President Bush after 9/11 was continued by Obama, under a different name but in no less deadly a fashion, and largely with drone-strikes. Since 2001, the US has militarily intervened in seven states in the Muslim world: Afghanistan, Iraq, Somalia, Yemen, Pakistan, Libya and Syria. These interventions have varied in intensity and scope, yet they have all had two consequences. They have pushed states towards collapse, and they have strengthened radical, Islamist movements, including the Taliban, al-Qaida and Islamic State. In no small measure, the West has created the terrorist threat it is fighting.

Even so, Washington has continued to differentiate between 'good' and 'bad' jihadis. 'Good' jihadis fight against 'bad' jihadis such as al-Qaida, or undesirable (i.e. anti-Western) governments. The following example illustrates how this works in practice. According to the news network Al-Jazeera, in summer 2014 the Americans followed a Saudi suggestion to open a new front against Assad's regime in the south of Syria. One unit associated with the Free Syrian Army, the Yarmouk Brigade, received weapons and special training via Jordan. The Brigade was allegedly 'moderate' and was supposed to oppose both regime troops and al-Qaida-sympathising Islamists in the north and east of Syria. However, to the chagrin of the Americans, video footage soon emerged showing the Yarmouk Brigade fighting alongside the Nusra Front, an al-Qaida offshoot. Worse still, the Brigade had handed the Nusra Front the state-of-the-art weapons systems they had just been given by Jordan, no doubt in exchange for good hard cash. Meanwhile the Baghdad government reiterated its now familiar complaint that IS in Iraq was using weapons originally supplied to 'good' Syrian Islamists by the US.

In Iraq, Washington supports the Shiites against Sunni jihadis, while in Syria, jihadis of the same stripe are encouraged by the US to wage war on the regime in Damascus. This schizophrenia has only strengthened Islamic State – first in Iraq, then in Syria, then back in Iraq. The Islamist movement in Iraq has its roots in the country's US-run prisons; later, in Syria, IS grew to a regional power, undisturbed by outside influences; finally, it launched a major offensive back into Iraq from Syria. At the start of June 2014, IS fighters tore down the border posts and declared the 'end of Sykes-Picot', the arbitrary 'lines in the sand' drawn to create the border between Iraq and Syria by Britain and France after World War I. Within a few weeks they had taken almost all western Iraq and conquered the second-largest Iraqi city, oil-rich Mosul; their territory extended almost to the borders of Baghdad.

The insurgents in Libya were also 'good' Islamists. Every sign of al-Qaida sympathies was played down by Washington. Only when US ambassador Chris Stevens was murdered by jihadis in September 2012 did the cry 'extremists!' go up, and with the usual consequences: inflamed rhetoric followed by military strikes. Washington now changed tack, applying the al-Qaida label where it did not fit – as it had during the fight against Sunni insurgents in occupied Iraq, though only a small proportion were actually members of al-Qaida. The truth was not important. What mattered was the equation *resistance* = *al-Qaida*, because this is what legitimised the Iraq occupation as an essential component of the war against terror. Of course, it also presented the Western public with a scapegoat for the unfolding disaster.

War Is Worth It

All new threats and challenges to the US-led intervention in the region meet the same, reflexive response: more weapons, more force. As the superpowers enter and exit one conflict zone after another, lessons are sometimes learned, but they concern mainly tactics or strategy. The use of violence *per se* is seldom questioned.

At the time of writing, for example, the party line is that large-scale ground offensives should be avoided in favour of drones and airstrikes, carried out in collaboration with (questionable) local allies. Is this simply to avoid casualties by risking more 'boots on the ground'? Or could there be other forces at work on US defence strategy?

Share prices in the largest US weapons company, Lockheed Martin, tripled between mid-2010 and mid-2014; they doubled between mid-2013 and mid-2014 alone. On 6 October 2014 media organisation Bloomberg reported:

> Led by Lockheed Martin Group (LTM), the biggest US defence companies are trading at record prices as shareholders reap rewards from escalating military conflicts around the world... investors see rising sales for makers of missiles, drones and other weapons as the US hits Islamic State fighters in Syria and Iraq... The US is also the biggest foreign military supplier to Israel, which waged a 50-day offensive against the Hamas Islamic movement in the Gaza Strip.

Germany's centre-right newspaper, the *Frankfürter Allgemeine Zeitung* was similarly bullish:

> the campaign against Islamic State is filling the order books of US weapons manufacturers and bringing them rich profits... The development of new weapons projects should also receive a boost. 'From the point of view of the defence industry, this is a perfect war,' said industry expert Richard Aboulafia from Market Research company Teal Group.

After the first American airstrikes on IS targets in Iraq in August 2014, former CIA Director Leon Panetta told *USA Today* that the nation was 'looking at a Thirty Year War.' His view, expounded in the book he was promoting at the time, was that this would be a war without territorial limits, extending beyond Islamic State to enfold emerging threats in Nigeria, Somalia, Yemen, Libya and wherever necessary, regardless of consequences for the affected regions and the people living there.

At the other end of the political spectrum, investigative journalist Glenn Greenwald has a similar view:

> At this point, it is literally inconceivable to imagine the US not at war. It would be shocking if that [an end to war] happened in our lifetime. US officials are now all but openly saying this. 'Endless War' is not dramatic rhetorical license but a precise description of America's foreign policy. It's not hard to see why. A state of endless war justifies ever-increasing state power and secrecy and a further erosion of rights. It also entails a massive transfer of public wealth to the 'homeland security' and weapons industry (which the US media deceptively calls the 'defence sector').

Caliph vs Caliph

In 2009, in a diplomatic telegram made public online by WikiLeaks, Secretary of State Hillary Clinton complained that Saudi Arabian donors were the biggest funding source for Sunni terrorist groups all over the world, including Islamic State. The funds were not supplied by the government, but by wealthy individuals and religious foundations within the country. The demands heard in Western capitals for Riyadh to block these financial transactions are naïve: any such move would meet with powerful resistance within Saudi Arabia. The US, Britain and other Western nations, continue to pay court to the Saudi regime, and persist against all evidence in seeing it as an ally in the fight against Sunni extremists. Meanwhile, Saudi preachers with audiences of millions openly call for the murder of 'heretic' Shiites.

Before 9/11, MI6 boss Richard Dearlove had a conversation with Prince Bandar bin Sultan, who was then Saudi ambassador to Washington and head of Saudi intelligence. 'The time is not far off in the Middle East, Richard,' said the Saudi diplomat, 'when it will be literally "God help the Shia". More than a billion Sunnis have simply had enough of them.'[14] Western governments play down the close ties – both ideological and financial – between Wahhabi state Islam and jihadis; like the Saudi government, they seem to believe the circle can be squared. On the one hand, they deploy Sunni jihadis to fight disagreeable governments, once in Afghanistan against the Soviets, now in Syria against Bashar al-Assad. On the other, they try to control the evil spirits they have let out of the bottle. In short, the lessons of 9/11 remain unlearned.

---

14 Patrick Cockburn, 'Iraq Crisis: How Saudi Arabia Helped ISIS To Take Over The North Of The Country'. *Independent*, 13 July 2014.

Prince Bandar was fired from his role as head of the Saudi secret service in 2014, because the government blamed him for strengthening Islamic State in Syria – a consequence of his strategy of using jihadis to try to topple Assad. (Prince Bandar is regarded as the instigator of the attack on Damascus in July 2012.) Yet there is very little indeed to choose between the world view of Wahhabism and the ideology of IS. The brutal approach of the new 'Caliphate' towards Shiites and other minorities, religious and/or ethnic (Kurds because they are not Arabs; Yezidis because they are neither Arabs nor Muslims), is very much in line with what the Saudi Wahhabis preach from their online pulpits, and what the Saudi state itself enforces within its borders through its feared *Mutawa*, or religious police.

Despite these ideological similarities, Islamic State is also at war with Saudi Arabia. When Abu Bakr al-Baghdadi proclaimed himself Caliph in Mosul on 29 June 2014, he was implicitly challenging Saudi Arabia's claim to leadership of the Sunni Islamic world. The nation calls itself 'the Caliphate of the Faithful' and the Saudi King bears the title 'Guardian of the Holy States' (referring to the pilgrim cities of Mecca and Medina).

Al-Qaida and Islamic State cannot be destroyed without attacking the roots and placing the Saudi regime itself under quarantine. Yet since Saudi Arabia is officially 'pro-West' and the world's largest producer of oil, this will almost certainly never happen. Even if the latest crop of extremists are defeated, the fighters will go underground, carry on under a different name or split up. Wahhabism, IS's spiritual bedrock, will still exist, as will the collapsed states of Syria and Iraq. All over the region, Sunnis and Shiites will continue to be at loggerheads.

As mentioned above, Islamic State emerged in Iraq, where al-Qaida had had little success in rallying the local population to its cause. In fact, many tribes along the Euphrates actively fought the terror organisation, supported with money and weapons from the US. Few Iraqi Sunnis shared al-Qaida's dream of a world-wide jihad against the crusaders. Their priority was to regain the power they had lost within Iraq. In any case, so many of al-Qaida's units were composed of foreign fighters that few Iraqis felt they had common cause with them.

This changed with IS, which at first was a purely Iraqi group, seeking and gaining power strictly within the borders of the nation. It relied on pre-existing structures built by al-Qaida, the Saddam regime or the Sunni tribes. Among its ranks were former officers, generals, secret service agents and soldiers who had served under Saddam. This gave them an edge in combat, intelligence and organisation. Funding from the Gulf States was another factor: it meant better weapons, more military success, more cash to pay the rank and file, and more recruits.

Down with the Romans!

If the war in Syria had not opened new fronts, IS would probably have remained within Iraq. But more and more Iraqi Shiites joined the Lebanese Hezbollah to fight on the side of Assad, fuelling the resentment of Sunnis, both in Iraq and Syria. They began to frame the conflict, not in terms of being pro- or anti-Assad, but of defending Sunni Islam against the heretical Shiites.

Its ranks swollen by outraged Sunnis, IS began to enlarge its sphere of activity, spreading from Iraq into Syria. It changed its name from 'Islamic State in Iraq' to 'Islamic State in Iraq and Sham'. In English, *Sham* is usually rendered as Syria, Greater Syria or the Levant, but the name (which, confusingly, is also used as a slang term for Damascus) has extra significance for devout

Muslims. Historically, Sham encompasses today's Syria, Lebanon, Israel/Palestine, and Jordan. Jerusalem, with its al-Aqsa Mosque commemorating the Prophet's ascent to Heaven, is the third holiest city in Islam, after Mecca and Medina. Damascus was the capital of the Umayyad Caliphate (661–750), the first Sunni empire. The city contains the graves of Saladin, the man who drove the crusaders from Jerusalem in 1187, and Ahmad ibn Taymiyya (1263–1328), an ultra-conservative law scholar who inspired the founders of Wahhabism. Many graves sacred to the Shiites also lie within Sham's territory, including the shrine to the Prophet's granddaughter, Zeinab, not far from Damascus.

Lastly, both Sunnis and Shiites – at least the most devout among them – believe that Sham will be the site of Armageddon, the Final Battle. According to one *hadith* (an account of the words and deeds of the Prophet), Muhammad declared: 'The Last Hour would not come until the Romans would land at al-A'maq or in Dabiq. An army consisting of the best (soldiers) of the people of the earth at that time will come from Medina (to counteract them).'

Al-A'maq and Dabiq are both situated north-east of Aleppo, on the Turkish border; 'Romans' denotes the Byzantines. According to the story, the Muslim army will meet a tremendous force of 42 armies, yet will triumph over the enemy. The Shiites, who only make up ten percent of Muslims, believe that after this final battle, the Mahdi, the Redeemer, will appear, and lead the devout into paradise. Radical Sunnis, meanwhile, interpret the *hadith* as a promise of a final victory over the infidel – including the Shiites.

It is therefore no surprise that Islamic State publishes an online magazine bearing the name of *Dabiq*. At its ideological heart is this powerful notion of an End-Time, followed by salvation.

The evolution of the group's name, from 'Islamic State in Iraq' to 'Islamic State in Iraq and Sham', and finally to 'Islamic State', reflects the rapid transformation that, within just a few years, turned an internal Iraqi organisation into a jihadi group speaking to the whole Sunni world. People in the West tend to label it as a terrorist organisation, and in so doing vastly underestimate its ambition. It is an Islamic state project that aims to tear down existing borders, and has outshone al-Qaida as a beacon for radicalised Sunnis.

Since 2010 their leader has been Ibrahim al-Badri, born in 1971 in Samarra, Iraq, a self-proclaimed Islamic scholar whose actual theological credentials are hazy. He supposedly attended Islamic seminars in Samarra and Baghdad, allegedly holds a diploma from an Islamic university in Samarra, and spent a few months in US custody in 2004. Little is known for certain about the man whose *nom de guerre* is Abu Bakr al-Baghdadi ('the one from Baghdad'). The name is loaded with symbolism. Abu Bakr was one of the first followers of Muhammad and His father-in-law. After Muhammad's death in 632, he ruled over the believers as a 'successor', or *caliph* in Arabic. Baghdad was the seat of the Abbasid Caliphate (750–1258), which succeeded the Umayyads in Damascus and founded a global empire stretching all the way from Spain to the borders of India.

Decoded, the symbolism of radical Sunnis sends this message: as the Abbasids succeeded the Umayyads, Islamic State is the successor to Saudi Arabia. IS has become the guardian of the true religion, just as the 7th-century Abu Bakr once preserved Muhammad's legacy. And IS addresses the entire Islamic world as its intellectual and spiritual centre – just as Baghdad once was. This is what gives IS an ideological edge. Al-Qaida stood for Bin Laden and 9/11. IS stands for the Caliphate, a lasting vision and source of identity. Al-Qaida was yesterday. IS marks today and tomorrow.

Advance into Syria

When Islamic State entered the Syrian civil war, it quickly overran the eastern regions previously controlled by other Islamist groups. On 9 April 2013, Abu Bakr al-Baghdadi declared the integration of IS with the Nusra Front, the Syrian branch of al-Qaida, though the next day this union was recanted by Nusra's leader, Abu Muhammad al-Julani. On 23 May 2013, Ayman al-Zawahiri, Osama Bin Laden's successor within al-Qaida, demanded that IS retreat to Iraq, triggering a conflict between the two organisations which cost the lives of around 6,000 people in the first half of 2014 alone. Better equipped and organised, IS defeated Nusra and its other rivals on almost all fronts.

Many radical, armed Islamists now defected to the winners, 'good jihadis' among them. Foreign and younger mujahideen in particular were attracted to the ruthlessness of IS, which launched a brutal assault on other Islamist groups, with car bombs, suicide bombers and assassinations.

IS's campaign in Syria was an economic as well as a military success. After conquering the Syrian oil fields around Deir Ezzor, they sold the black gold to the Assad regime, to customers in Turkey, and finally, from the summer of 2014, to Iraq as well. The further into Syria his forces penetrated, the more credible seemed al-Baghdadi's claim to be the supreme commander of all jihadis in Syria, Iraq and beyond. As ruler of all the devout, a Caliph could not be confined within a single state; in early 2014, therefore, IS launched its surprise attack on Iraq. The Caliphate was declared in Mosul on 29 June.

Abu Bakr al-Baghdadi – or Caliph Ibrahim – is fixated on consolidating his own power, an agenda he has pursued with extreme ruthlessness. He quickly showed himself adept at using religious symbolism to stoke the emotions and mobilise his followers. It was no accident that his Caliphate was declared on 29 June, the first day of Ramadan, the month of fasting. On the first Friday of that holy month, 4 July 2014, he delivered his first sermon in the Nuri Mosque in Mosul. According to Dr Stephan Rosiny of the GIGA Institute of Middle Eastern Studies, even Abu Bakr's opening movements were part of the show:

> Because of a war injury suffered in the jihad battle, he ascended to the pulpit with a limp. There, he first cleaned his mouth with a twig, a devout gesture among Salafis, before putting into his mouth the verses of the Quran – 'God's words' – with which he strengthened his address, delivered in classical high Arabic. He was dressed in a black turban and cloak, as was Muhammad, supposedly, when he recaptured Mecca in the year 630.[15]

The black flag of IS and its fighters' fondness for black clothing all played on this idea of re-conquest. Furthermore, black uniforms and flags were part of the courtly etiquette of the Abbasids in the eighth century, and thus serve as reminders of Islam's golden age. Even Abu Bakr's valuable wrist watch, the source of much online ridicule, could be seen as legitimate 'spoils of war': 'On the whole, he presented himself humbly as an equal among

15 Stefan Rosiny, 'Des Kalifen neue Kleider: Der Islamische Staat in Irak und Syrien' (The Caliph's New Clothes: Islamic State in Syria and Iraq), GIGA Focus Nahost, August 2014

equals who had taken on the heavy burden of the Caliph. "Obey me, as I obey God and his messenger. If I do not obey God and his messenger, you do not have to obey me." With this rhetorical phrase, which he took from Abu Bakr's inaugural speech as the First Caliph in 632, he distanced himself from the power-hungry despots of the region.'[16] At the same time, he followed Salafist tradition in forbidding any worship of a human as a holy being.

The 'Manchester United' of Jihad

Islamic State's triumphal procession through the Sunni region of Iraq in June 2014 could not have happened without the Iraqi army. Most of the approximately 100,000 soldiers along the front-lines simply fled, leaving their top-of-the-range American weapons behind, including tanks and planes. Even before this, Islamic State had intercepted several weapons deliveries in Syria, intended for 'good' jihadis by the US and the Gulf States. In September 2014, the *New York Times* estimated the worth of the weapons lost to IS at several hundred million dollars; this booty was instrumental in turning the group into a major regional power. The idea of the Caliphate, so attractive to radical Islamists, alongside the promise of conquest and robbery and a war against the pampered Gulf States and the hated West, combined to give IS a cultic appeal. It seemed the winning team, the Bayern Munich or the Manchester United of jihad. Just as these teams have followers worldwide, IS drew thousands of fighters from North Africa, Europe, the Caucasus, the Far East and all over the Middle East towards its heartlands in Syria and Iraq.

It is hard to blame the Iraqi soldiers for their flight. The Iraqi

---

16 *Ibid.*

army is riddled with corruption, with every rank from corporal to general for sale, and it was often the officers who deserted first. Why would an ordinary soldier risk his life for $60 a month, in the service of an inept and corrupt government in Baghdad?

The IS fighters had no such motivational problems. They were in a win-win situation. If they killed their enemies, they would receive 'bonus points' counting towards their ascent to the seventh heaven, the highest level of paradise. If they died as 'martyrs', they'd get there straight away, greeted as fearless heroes by (ideally blonde) virgins, their eyes aglow with passion... The power of such erotic visions over the imaginations of men living in the sexually repressed societies of the Middle East can hardly be over-estimated. Among IS fighters, the rape of 'infidel' women, including in the form of forced prostitution, is common practice. For young men forbidden under normal circumstances to have sex outside marriage, and who are often too poor to marry, such opportunities proved all too enticing.

It is part of IS's combat strategy to broadcast its warriors' contempt for death. During their advance through Iraq, it was sometimes enough merely to phone the town authorities or the barracks to say they were on their way. This alone would prompt panic, flight and surrender. The decapitation videos that were doing the rounds on the internet sowed further terror. Mosul was taken with almost no resistance. The reason was simple: fear.

In general, those Sunnis who are willing to embrace the ideology of IS and acknowledge its right to rule have nothing to fear, while members of religious minorities are called upon to convert to Islam. Christians, if they are lucky, are given the option of paying a fixed 'head tax', with non-payment punishable by death. Shiites who fall into the hands of IS are frequently shot on the spot, as are government soldiers or Kurdish fighters, often in their hundreds.

Daily Life in the Caliphate

Meanwhile, day-to-day life in areas controlled by IS appeared on the surface largely normal. Universities and schools remained open. Community services such as waste disposal continued to run. There were soup kitchens for the army, and the needy received support. Taxes were collected, and conscription introduced. The territory was divided into provinces, and a 'financial equalisation scheme' redistributed wealth to poorer areas. 'Caliph Ibrahim' publicly called for jurists and judges, engineers, administrators and doctors to come and help establish the new state. And they were offered relatively decent wages: there was no shortage of money, with the oil trade bringing in large sums of foreign currency. Contributions from rich individuals and religious foundations in the Gulf States swelled the coffers further. Smuggling supplied yet another lucrative source of funds, not to mention ransoms and extortion.

In total, six million people lived in IS-controlled areas. Its zone of influence stretched from the outskirts of Aleppo to the borders of Baghdad. At the time of writing the capital city of the Caliphate remains, despite months of bombardment, the Syrian desert city of Raqqa. At its height, according to the American secret services, IS had up to 30,000 active fighters; other sources spoke of more than 50,000. At least as many 'state' functionaries ensured the smooth administration of the Caliphate. Fighters were paid monthly wage of between $200 and $600, with administrators earning $300 on average and senior managers up to $2000.

The exact command structure remains opaque. It is said that 'Caliph Ibrahim' has two representatives, one responsible for Syria, the other for Iraq; that there is a 'leadership council' made up of a small group of the leader's trusted colleagues. A 'cabinet' of technocrats and managers concerns itself with finances, security, prisoners, the recruitment of fighters and, not least, the strikingly professional handling of the media. Finally, 'regional councils' serve as points of contact, taking care of both military and civil operations. Many former officers of the Saddam regime are active in such 'councils'.

Militarily, IS favours small raiding parties, travelling in a Toyota 4x4 mounted with machine guns or grenade launchers. These units can be quickly cobbled together, with communication mostly via mobile phones or messenger services like Snapchat and Telegram – though IS is also thought to possess its own secure communication network. Its fighters, benefiting from maximum speed and surprise, shoot to clear the way for the following units. These guerrilla tactics give them a significant advantage over conventional armies.

What IS understands by education, meanwhile, is clear from the following document (translated from the original Arabic):

Diwan al-Ta'lim (Department of Education)

My Lord! Increase my knowledge
ISLAMIC STATE:
A Caliphate in the Spirit of the Prophets
Declaration number 006

IN THE NAME OF THE MOST BENEFICENT
God be praised for His support of Islam and Muslims and be He praised for the hollows of disbelief and the non-believers. Revere Him and bow to Him, Muhammad the most exquisite of prophets. Allah prays for him and for all prophets and their disciples until the end of time.

Proclamation to all faculties of the university in Mosul, to all professors, lecturers, colleagues and employees.

After studying the present situation and after examining the affairs of the Muslims and what the general interest requires, IS' Diwan al-Ta'aleem has decided on the following:

- All professors, lecturers, colleagues and employees of the university in Mosul are required to perform their work regularly, starting on **24 Dhu al-Hijjah 1435 AH / 18 October 2014**. In particular, they are required to do everything necessary to ensure that university examinations take place.

The following colleges and departments are not legitimate according to Shari'a, and have been shut down:
- College of human rights, political sciences and fine arts.
- Departments of archaeology, physical education, and philosophy.
- Department of Tourism and Hotel Management.

The following subjects not conforming to Shari'a have also been cancelled:
- Democracy, culture, freedom, rights.
- Fiction and theatre in the English and French language; translations in general.
- Themes of nationality, ethnicity, history and state boundaries will form no part of the university's teaching.

Professors, lecturers, and teachers are required to observe the following:

- the segregation of men and women, according to Shari'a.
- the replacement of the term 'Republic of Iraq' with 'Islamic State'
- the replacement of the term 'Ministry of Higher Education' with 'Department of Education'
- Diwan al-Ta'aleem.

THIS PROCLAMATION IS AN ORDER AND IS LEGALLY BINDING. INFRINGEMENTS WILL BE PUNISHED.

'God always prevails in whatever be His purpose: but most people know it not' Qur'an 12:21.
Diwan al-Ta'aleem.
Signed, Dhu al-Qarnein[17]

Dhu al-Qarnein is a pseudonym whose literal translation is 'the two-horned one'. Once used to describe Alexander the Great in Arabic, it is code for 'we will have a mighty Empire'. The tone is typical of radical Islamists. Extreme religious piety is used to whitewash a world-view that demands absolute conformity and submission.

Scorched Earth

How should we deal with the threat of Islamic State and militant Islamism? There are no simple answers. The growth of extremist groups is payback for the illegal and wrong-headed US-led

17 Part of the text can be viewed at: http://www.aymennjawad.org/15946/aspects-of-islamic-state-is-administration-in

invasion of Iraq in 2003, for the ensuing collapse of the Iraqi state, and for the war in Syria, which is at once a civil and a proxy war. The failed attempt to use 'good' jihadis to bring down Bashar al-Assad created a power vacuum which IS triumphantly filled. There is little to suggest that a change of strategy is on the cards. Officially, the West continues to pursue its goal of regime change in Syria, in the deluded hope that the Baghdad government will somehow help defuse the tensions between Sunnis and Shiites – even though their policies are part of the problem. And the airstrikes go on...

The damage that has been wreaked in Iraq and Syria by Western intervention is colossal, and perhaps irreparable. It is hard to discern even the outlines of a possible solution. Perhaps the entire region has go up in flames before Washington grasps that a rethink is needed. At the very least, instead of bending over backwards to keep Israel happy, the US must ditch its inflexible stance towards Iran and start negotiating. The West must finally accept the Shiite state as a powerful actor in the region, and a valuable counterweight against Sunni extremism. President Trump's recent visit to the Middle East gives little cause for hope.

Meanwhile, the Israeli government sets itself ever more rigidly against the foundation of a Palestinian state. Jerusalem's Temple Mount, where the Wailing Wall borders the Al-Aqsa Mosque, has become an increasingly dangerous flashpoint. Muslims are denied access to the mosque, while groups of Jews are escorted under armed guard (arranged by ultra-nationalists in the Israeli parliament) onto the grounds of the mosque, where they are encouraged to say their prayers at high volume. It may not be so very long before the extremists of the Jewish State are indistinguishable from those of the Islamic State.

At the same time, the monarchs in the Gulf States are shaking in their boots. They know only too well that Islamist extremism poses an existential threat if its seeds take root among their own populations. The spirits they have summoned with their Wahhabism could one day see them toppled from their thrones.

In this chaotic situation, the best hope for Western governments is to deal with all protagonists, including Russia and China. Yet Washington continues to follow the logic of hegemony, rather than seeking a balance of powers. The goal is the political and economic dominance of the US. In the end, this lack of pragmatism may well accelerate its downfall still further.

We Support You, But We Know You Won't Win

A military solution – the surrender or total destruction of Islamic State, for instance – is not realistic. Far more likely is an ongoing armed conflict that swells the weapons industry still further. Recent history furnishes not a single example of a regular army defeating a guerrilla force, and there is little to suggest that the case of IS will be any different.

Washington continues to claim that there will be no 'boots on the ground', but in the medium term this policy is likely to be reversed. Airstrikes alone can produce only selective, localised damage. Throughout 2016, the US dropped some 26,171 bombs – or three bombs an hour, 24 hours a day – principally on IS targets on Syria and Iraq.[18] By way of comparison, there were almost 2,000 strikes made daily throughout the Vietnam War. At the same time, the Iraqi army continues to receive training, so that its soldiers can be sent off to fight against IS. At the start of 2015

18 Medea Benjamin. 'America Dropped 26,171 Bombs in 2016.' *Guardian*. 9 January 2017.

there were over 3,500 American military personnel deployed in Iraq, officially in advisory or training roles. Yet these efforts did little to hinder IS's triumphant advance.

'The Central Intelligence Agency has run guns to insurgencies across the world during its 67-year history — from Angola to Nicaragua to Cuba. The continuing CIA effort to train Syrian rebels is just the latest example of an American president becoming enticed by the prospect of using the spy agency to covertly arm and train rebel groups,' wrote the *New York Times* in October 2014. Even so, the newspaper continued, 'an internal CIA study has found that it rarely works.'[19] According to the report, Obama commissioned the study (which remained classified) in order to evaluate the wisdom of military intervention in Syria. Comparable CIA interventions in the past, according to the analysis, had only ever had a 'minimal impact on the long-term outcome of a conflict'.

Nevertheless, in April 2013 the President gave the order to begin training Syrian insurgents at a military base in Jordan. Later, this intervention was expanded, with the aim of preparing 5,000 rebels in Saudi Arabia each year for the fight against Islamic State. The *New York Times* report went on: 'The fact that the CIA took a dim view of its own past efforts to arm rebel forces fed Mr Obama's reluctance to begin the covert operation' or to deploy American boots on the ground. It did not, however, stop him from continuing to send 'good' jihadis to fight Assad, thereby hastening the destruction of Syria.

Two weeks later, the American linguist and social critic Noam Chomsky wrote: 'President Obama should call our country's

---

19 Mark Mazetti, 'C.I.A. Study of Covert Aid Fueled Skepticism About Helping Syrian Rebels'. *New York Times*, 14 Oct 2014 (https://www.nytimes.com/2014/10/15/us/politics/cia-study-says-arming-rebels-seldom-works.html)

history of supporting insurgents abroad for what it is: US-backed terrorism.'[20] He analysed the measures taken to destabilise Angola, Nicaragua and Cuba, pointing out that the arming and financing of the terrorist army UNITA under the leadership of Jonas Savimbi in Angola alone resulted in the deaths of more than 1.5 million people, according to a UN investigation in 1989. 'Washington,' Chomsky wrote, 'has emerged as the world champion in generating terror.' He cited former CIA analyst Paul Pillar, who warned that airstrikes in Syria would encourage anti-Western resentment and lead the Islamists of the Nusra front and IS to drop their differences and band together. Chomsky also quoted journalist and ex-CIA agent Graham Fuller: 'The United States did not plan the formation of ISIS [...] but its destructive interventions in the Middle East and the War in Iraq were the basic causes of the birth of ISIS.'

Islamic State's military leadership consists mostly of Saddam's old generals, who still have a bone to pick with the British and Americans. They scarcely bother to conceal their desire to tempt the West into a ground offensive: they know that embarking on an unwinnable war (c.f. Afghanistan, the occupation of Iraq) would mire Western governments in a political morass. This is what explains the decapitations of British and American hostages. They are intended to provoke widespread outrage and increase the domestic political pressure to 'do something'.

The terror attacks in Europe could be interpreted as part of the same strategy. For Islamic State, a foreign invasion would afford a welcome opportunity for 'Caliph Ibrahim' to cast himself as a modern, crusader-defying Saladin, and call for a global jihad

20 Noam Chomsky, 'The Long Shameful History of US Terrorism'. In These Times, Nov 3 2014. (http://inthesetimes.com/article/17311/noam_chomsky_the_worlds_greatest_terrorist_campaign)

against the infidels. Undoubtedly IS would pay a high price in blood – but with its guerrilla forces impossible to finally 'defeat', its leadership could claim victory through mere survival. Meanwhile, another large-scale military intervention in an Islamic country would unleash violent emotions world-wide.

Guns For 'Good' Kurds

Western military intervention can be justified when it helps stop the advance of extremist groups into new territory, or when it is needed to support its opponents – for instance, the Kurds in northern Iraq and Syria. In late 2014 the northern Syrian town of Kobani on the Turkish border was besieged by Islamic State, whose forces were at the time advancing towards Erbil, capital of Iraq's autonomous Kurdish region. Targeted US airstrikes around Kobani and Erbil inflicted severe damage, killing between ten and thirty fighters each day. For the first time, IS was put on the defensive. Intervention sometimes works, but only when its goals are clearly circumscribed, and limited to a specific territory.

After these battles, Kurdish fighters were able to help persecuted minorities in northern Iraq, including the Yezidis, escape certain death at the hands of IS, by creating an escape corridor towards Syria and northern Iraq. Western governments began to provide the northern Iraqi Kurds with military training and light weapons. Yet, as we shall see, this apparently unobjectionable operation has opened a political can of worms.

Like the Palestinians, the Kurds are a people without a state. After World War I, the colonial powers of Britain and France ignored their claim to independence. Instead they were divided across four nations: Syria, Turkey, Iraq and Iran. It is the

Kurds of northern Iraq who have gained most from the post-2003 upheavals. In their autonomous region, they are *de facto* independent, though they have avoided making a formal declaration of independence so as not to provoke their next-door neighbour, Turkey.

Thanks to their oil wealth, the Kurdish areas are economically booming. The vast majority of their oil is bought by Turkey, whose companies are some of the largest investors in northern Iraq (this despite Turkey's treatment of its own Kurdish people). The current leader of the region is Masoud Barzani. His chief opponent is Jalal Talabani, who, thanks to his close relations with Washington, held the largely token office of Iraqi President between 2005 and 2014.

The Kurds are a far from homogenous group. They are composed of numerous factions with widely divergent interests that have at times led to violent conflict. In very simple terms, there are two rival political streams: the old, tribal-feudalism, whose most important representatives are Barzani and Talabani; and a 'social revolutionary' current, which rejects traditional tribal and religious structures, and is represented by the Kurdish Workers' Party (PKK).

Officially, the West is now delivering weapons to the Peshmerga. The name means 'they who face death', and has become a catch-all term for Kurdish fighters in any given conflict area. Currently, the word mainly denotes the armed forces of the Kurdish autonomous region in Northern Iraq. Yet many of the fighters taking on IS are members of the PKK, which is outlawed as a terrorist organisation in both Turkey and Europe.

The war between the Turkish army and the PKK in the southeast of Turkey has been raging since 1984 and has so far claimed at least 60,000 lives. A few years ago Ankara formally agreed a treaty with PKK leader Abdullah Öcalan, who has been imprisoned in Turkey since 1999. This was meant to guarantee the Kurds certain rights of self-rule, especially in the south-east of the country, but from the Kurdish point of view, Ankara has not made good its promises.

After an attack on a Turkish village on the border with Syria by Islamic State in July 2015, President Erdogan's government's first reaction was to launch airstrikes on IS targets in Syria. At the same time, however, under the cover of combatting 'all terrorist organisations', Turkey attacked PKK camps in Iraq and then Syria. The general confusion and unrest had afforded an opportunity for the Turkish government, alarmed by gains being made against IS by Kurdish forces in Syria and Iraq, to curb their ambitions. These events signalled the end of the ceasefire with the PKK.

The West continued to supply weapons to the Peshmerga, irrespective of the fact that the PKK was now once again at war with Turkey and classed as a terrorist organisation. There were two possible ways of rectifying this anomaly: either stop sending weapons to 'terrorists', or take the PKK off the terror list. Instead, governments stubbornly adhered to the official line – that all weapons were going to the 'good' Kurds, the Peshmerga.

Unlike the Iraqi Kurds, the Kurds of northern Syria do not occupy a coherent territory; they are scattered over three 'cantons'. The smallest canton is the central one, which contains Kobani. Islamic State's attack was a deliberate attempt to drive a wedge between the regions, an aim with which the Turkish government were highly sympathetic, since the largest Kurdish political party in Syria, the Democratic Union (PYK), is a branch of the PKK. Turkey allowed very few Kurds to cross the border into Syria – though token numbers of Iraqi Kurdish Peshmerga were let through in order to curry favour with Barzani. From the Turkish point of view, the Kurds of Northern Iraq are valued partners, while those in their own country present a security risk. The successful defence of Kobani, with the help of American airstrikes, was a development Ankara had not foreseen. Nor was it welcome, as being likely to produce a surge of support for the PKK and PYK.

Erdogan had been among the first to break with Assad when the war in Syria began, despite their long-standing personal friendship. It seems that he hoped to strengthen Turkey's influence in the Middle East as mentor to a future Sunni government in Damascus. For this miscalculation, Turkey paid two high penalties. One was the 1.5 million refugees who came into the country. The other was the new neighbour in the south: Islamic State. The regime was well aware that IS could cause Turkey significant political and economic damage: a few more terrorist attacks in Istanbul or the tourist centres of the Antalya region would suffice. In response to this danger, the Erdogan launched a military campaign against Islamic State in July 2015 – though it was waged with conspicuously less urgency than the one against the PKK. Islamic State continued to recruit within Turkey, and its wounded fighters were treated in Turkish hospitals. Close contacts between the Turkish secret service and IS, specifically with ex-Saddam people, was maintained.

At the time of writing, the future of Islamic State is unclear. Militarily, it is on the back foot, its territory shrinking. Three years after al-Baghdadi was proclaimed Caliph, Mosul appears on the brink of recapture by the Iraqi army. IS's ability to field conventional – or semi-conventional – armies is diminished, and panicked predictions of the Caliphate spreading over the entire Middle East will not be fulfilled any time soon. Yet it is equally certain that its guerrilla forces will not suffer a definitive defeat; such a defeat is inconceivable, a logical impossibility. Islamist extremism will not just melt away. Whether IS continues to operate under the same name, or merges with other groups such as al-Qaida, or its fighters coalesce into a new structure, it will retain its capacity to commit acts of terrorism, both in the Middle East and elsewhere. A world where violent Islamist extremism has no constituency would be a world without hundreds of thousands of disenfranchised, impoverished Muslims who blame the West for their problems. Such a world remains, even to the most optimistic of prognosticators, difficult to imagine.

UNHOLY ALLIANCES

Western policy-makers are largely blind to the causes and the complexity of social change in the Middle East. They continue to believe in the panacea of military intervention. They support vicious but allegedly 'moderate' Arab regimes – for instance, in the Gulf States and in Egypt – because they are pro-Western and seem to promise stability. They proclaim democracy, freedom and human rights, yet they accept election results only if the winner is to their liking.

When Hamas won the election in the Palestinian territories is 2006, the regions were boycotted and isolated. Since then, there have been no further elections, in case Hamas win again. When the elected Muslim Brotherhood were ousted from power in Egypt in a coup in 2013, there were a few voices raised in concern in Western capitals, but not many. The same chorus of indifference greeted the military putsch against the Islamic Salvation Front in Algeria in 1991, shortly before their predicted election victory.

Egypt's new ruler, Field Marshal Sisi, is fawned over by the West, who see him as a vital intermediary between Israel and the Palestinians. Without Riyadh's approval, there would probably be no President Sisi: Egypt is dependent on Saudi money. The Wahhabi regime gave the green light to the putsch out of fear that the Muslim Brotherhood, markedly more moderate than they are, might become a dangerous rival in the region. Not to mention their anxiety as to what might happen if their own citizens should be inspired by the success of the Arab Spring.

Any country that defies the West – Iran, Syria, Saddam's Iraq, Gaddafi's Libya, Putin's Russia – is punished with sanctions. Again and again these are imposed, in the vain hope that they will bring about regime change. Yet nowhere have sanctions achieved regime change. If a state implodes as a result of Western military intervention, the Americans launch undeclared, dirty wars against 'terrorists', fought largely by mercenaries (as in Yemen, Somalia, Libya, Iraq and Syria). Drone strikes are a key part of the strategy. They were Obama's weapon of choice, and Trump shows no sign of changing course. No one really knows how many casualties these – for the most part officially-denied – operations have caused. In Afghanistan alone, during the thirteen years of occupation to 2014, over 10,000 people are said to have died. Most were civilians – or 'collateral damage'.

If nothing else, their experiences in Somalia, Afghanistan, Iraq and elsewhere have taught the Americans something about the expense and risks of sending in ground troops, and the difficulty of keeping the support of their own population. Hence the perennial demand for 'solidarity' from the likes of Britain and Germany, the aim being not just to keep military costs down, but to shift political responsibility. Washington's ideal is a delegated war, with European partners and 'good' jihadis taking up the franchise, so to speak. The idea has sold well, not least in Germany, where President Gauck opened the 2014 Munich Security Conference by declaring that his country was ready to 'take on greater responsibility' and 'make a more substantial contribution' to global affairs.

A Responsibility to Bomb Libya

The testing ground for the 'delegated war' was Libya, and the military operation to remove Gaddafi. On 18 March 2011, the very night after the passing of UN Resolution 1973 (which cites a 'responsibility to protect' Libyan civilians), British and French planes began to bombard Gaddafi's troops, preventing their invasion of Benghazi. As mentioned earlier, Moscow and Beijing were caught unawares: they had not grasped that the West would interpret the Resolution as *carte blanche* to remove Gaddafi. Leadership of the Benghazi operation, which continued into late summer, was assumed by Britain and France, in close consultation with the US, whose own role was formally confined to offering logistical support.

In September 2011, the British Prime Minister David Cameron told a cheering crowd in Benghazi: 'Your city was an inspiration to the world as you threw off a dictator and chose freedom.' Was the Libyan operation really a shining example of a successful intervention, unsullied by self-interest?

Gaddafi's fall was the result of his insistently anti-Western politics. His leading role in the African Union was a thorn in the Americans' side: he had used it to thwart every bid to build American military bases in Africa. Access to Libyan resources also played its part. Unlike in Iraq, exploration rights in Libya, the twelfth largest oil producer in the world, had been granted mainly to Chinese rather than to British and American oil companies. The Russians, who had also had good business relations with Gaddafi, were the other big losers after he was removed.

Like Bashar al-Assad or Saddam Hussein, Gaddafi was a feudal leader, who since 1969 had presided over a nepotistic and repressive system. The beginnings of a civil society existed in the capital, Tripoli, and in the city of Benghazi. Throughout the rest of the country, though, like much of the Middle East, clans and tribes formed the bedrock of the social structure.

What happened after Gaddafi's fall is what happens whenever

a power vacuum needs to be filled. Without a strong central government, a battle for power – and a share of oil income – broke out, among rival tribal and regional militias. Violent Islamist groups entered the mix. Murder became part of everyday politics, as the various militias carried out kidnappings, imprisonments without trial and systematic torture, executions, ransom demands and extortion. In different circumstances, Libya's oil wealth might provide every one of its six million citizens with a standard of living equal to that in Switzerland, but centuries-old social structures, attitudes and practices, including the blood feud, proved stronger than reason.

Gaddafi himself had relied heavily on militias, sometimes made up of mercenaries recruited from the Sahel and western sub-Saharan Africa. After his demise, these now unemployed mercenaries returned to their homelands with their weapons, and looked for new opportunities and partners. The dramatic increase in terrorist attacks by Boko Haram in Nigeria since 2012, as well as the advance of Tuareg rebels in northern Mali, can be traced back to these marauding ex-mercenaries. They are part of the fall-out from Western intervention in Libya. In 2013, France felt the need to send soldiers into its former colony, Mali.

French troops succeeded in preventing the rebels from advancing further towards the capital, though they were unable to eradicate them in the north of the country. In other words, having first helped to topple Gaddafi in Libya, France then had to send soldiers into another country in order to deal with the consequences. Paris had indeed 'taken on more responsibility', to use President Gauck's phrase.

Libya is yet another example of the devastating consequences that follow Western military intervention. Some argue that it is hardly the fault of America or Europe if the newly 'freed' people of one country or another proceed to tear each other apart. This argument fails to take account of the facts. Again and again, as night follows day, the attempt to 'democratise' a feudal order using military force has created a power vacuum that is quickly filled by violent groups, Islamist or otherwise. The collapse of the state and the rule of militias invariably ensue.

Wars and Demons

I have suggested that military intervention can be justified when it has a specific, well-defined purpose: the airstrikes on IS targets, for example, which prevented the massacre of Kurds in Kobani and Erbil. Yet it is seldom that the interests of an external power and those of a local group fall into alignment – and when they do, then only briefly. Many Afghans were glad when the Taliban were ousted in 2001, though joy gave way to disbelief when the old warlords who had brought so much calamity to their country returned to power. For their part, the Americans seemed unperturbed. Although the US had fought against the Taliban within Afghanistan, it chose not to act against its supporters in Pakistan. Similarly, those Iraqis who welcomed the fall of Saddam were dismayed at the foreign occupation that followed. For all that the Americans had wanted to prevent Iran from profiting from the end of Saddam's regime, that's exactly what happened, as the new Shiite government in Baghdad worked closely with Tehran in going after their Sunni compatriots.

Libya, Afghanistan, Iraq, Syria... All these foreign interventions have been attempts by the West to enthrone a new leader after their own taste. Always they have claimed that the current rulers – the Taliban, Saddam, Gaddafi, Assad – are not only evil, crazy, fanatic and dangerous, but also hated by their own people. In

Libya, intervention ensured the success of an uprising that would not have been strong enough to challenge Gaddafi on its own, and which brought ruin in its wake. Meanwhile, the reflux of mercenaries destabilised still further the Sahel and sub-Saharan African states, among them Cameroon, Niger and Chad. In Afghanistan, with the occupying forces withdrawn, at least officially, the Taliban seems likely to rise once again to dominance. In Iraq, the Americans drove the ruling Sunnis, who now found themselves at the mercy of a Shiite central government intent on revenge, straight into the hands of the insurgency from which 'Islamic State' was born. Lastly, had it not been for the determination of the West (or the 'Friends of the Syrian People') to bring down Assad at any price, IS would never have found a foothold in Syria.

The Path to the Putsch

In Egypt, events took a different course. The mass protests in Tahir Square in February 2011 prompted the military – *de facto* power holders since 1952 – to demand the resignation of the ruler of almost 30 years, Hosni Mubarak. But, despite the removal of the king, the protests gave rise to no new order. The foundations simply did not exist. It is worth hammering the point home: no Arabic country today possesses a middle class large or powerful enough to support more than a superficial democratic transformation. Not to mention the lack of such other preconditions as a plural society, tolerance for diversity, and respect for the rule of law. 'Generation Facebook', whose young, open-minded members played such an important role in the protests, were quickly pushed aside. Western-oriented, liberal politicians had no power base beyond a few middle-class districts in Cairo, and in any case were unable to set aside their petty rivalries to create a secular coalition. Throughout the Arab world, patronage trumps politics: parties are chosen not for their policies, but for the favours they promise their supporters.

With the fall of Mubarak, the hour of the Muslim Brotherhood had struck. Founded in 1928, they became a counter-force to Wahhabism across the Islamic world. In Egypt they had been outlawed for decades, though under Mubarak they were tolerated. Traditionally they were strong in universities and professional organisations, where their candidates would present themselves as 'Independent' or 'Not belonging to any Party'.

The Muslim Brotherhood have their origins as an anti-colonial party; later, in the Cold War era, they fought against the influence of the USA and USSR. They also stood up to unjust rulers and corruption, and promulgated an ideal of social justice. For millions of Egyptians, they supplied concrete aid in their daily struggle to survive. In Egypt, more than half the population lives on or below the bread line, and the state has never provided even a minimum of welfare for its citizens. The Muslim Brotherhood set up soup kitchens and supported people in the direst need. It is no wonder that, in the first free presidential elections in 2012, the Muslim Brotherhood candidate, Muhammad Morsi, took almost 52 percent of the vote.

It was a Pyrrhic victory. Behind the scenes, the army and the business elite remained the true wielders of power. In addition to numerous mutual financial interests, they shared the view that the Muslim Brotherhood were a vulgar, dangerous rabble. Over the decades, the army top brass had built up a veritable business empire that spanned the food industry, the tourist sector and real estate covering entire city districts. The business elite, too, had become fantastically wealthy compared with the average Egyptian citizen, and they married their sons and daughters to the children of generals and colonels. Neither group were inclined to share their privileges. From the outset, they were determined to bring Morsi down.

Two days before Morsi was elected President, the Supreme Court, dominated by judges still loyal to Mubarak, annulled the 2011/12 parliamentary elections, which the Muslim Brotherhood had clearly won, and dissolved parliament on the basis of an alleged procedural error. Obstructions of this kind continued after Morsi assumed office as President. He was not briefed adequately on the state of the nation's finances, this information being treated as 'classified' by the elite. The judiciary frustrated every attempt on the part of the Muslim Brotherhood to change the law. Policemen stayed at home en masse, and the crime rate soared. The media, in the pockets of the elite, blamed the Muslim Brotherhood for everything, above all for the country's economic woes, as though the economic know-how of the generals extended beyond knowing how to enrich themselves. In the sixteen months between the fall of Mubarak and Morsi taking office, the army-controlled transition government had managed to spend their way through half of Egypt's foreign exchange reserves. Yet if they had systematically plundered the treasury, they had also been careful to scatter financial rewards among the people, mainly in the form of subsidies for bread, petrol and electricity. The message: it is the army that truly loves the Egyptians.

The elites simply waited for their chance to bring down Morsi. The Muslim Brotherhood did not see the trap. After decades of working outside the law, they found it hard to make the transition to an open, transparent style of politics. Perhaps their biggest mistake was to make no effort to attract those who hadn't voted for them. Instead the party retreated into solipsism, and came to appear incompetent and out of their depth. The unrealistic expectations of many Egyptians that Morsi would transform their lives overnight rapidly ebbed, leaving in their wake feelings of anger and disappointment, which the media were only to happy to stoke.

When the Muslim Brotherhood forced through a new constitution granting them greater executive powers in January 2013, the first mass protests began in Cairo, before spreading to the rest of the country. In June, hundreds of thousands of demonstrators demanded Morsi's resignation. On 3 July, the army stepped in to depose him, and threw him in prison along with other Muslim Brotherhood leaders.

Thought Police

Violent clashes now broke out between Morsi supporters and security forces, reaching their bloody peak in August. The ruthless new army leadership, under supreme commander Abd al-Fattah al-Sisi, ordered the shelling of a Muslim Brotherhood-led protest camp in Cairo, killing between 1,000 and 1,500 people. Violence in Egypt has been rising ever since, with more and more attacks carried out on soldiers, politicians and government buildings, especially on the Sinai Peninsula, where radical Islamists had been fighting the government for many years. These groups had no connection to the Muslim Brotherhood, but such details did not interest the new regime, and in September they declared it a terrorist organisation, banning it and seizing its assets. Almost the entire membership of the Muslim Brotherhood was arrested and hundreds of national, regional and local leaders, including Muhammad Morsi and Muhammad Badiyyah, the Muslim Brotherhood's second-in-command, were condemned to death. Soup kitchens and other welfare activities run by the

Brotherhood were forced to close down, threatening the survival of many Egyptians across the country.

This set the final course towards civil war and violence. The Muslim Brotherhood have a tribal electorate of about 35 to 40 percent. To imply that more than a third of the population were 'terrorists' was, to put it mildly, inflammatory. The fact that many other Egyptians supported the brutal actions of the military, having fallen for their jingoistic propaganda, does not mitigate the breathtaking irresponsibility of the new regime's treatment of the Muslim Brotherhood.

General Sisi had himself promoted to Field Marshal and was elected President in May 2014, apparently with 96.31 percent of the vote (on a turnout that even official sources admit was less than 50 percent). Despite the obvious manipulation of the figures and the questionable conditions surrounding Sisi's ascent to power, the EU mission, which had travelled to the Nile for the purposes of observing the election, declared that it had been 'democratic and free'.

Once Sisi was in power, the army/government went after its opponents with all possible force, under the guise of 'fighting terrorism', attacking not just the Muslim Brotherhood, but also democratic activists and protesting students. Since the universities had developed into bastions of the anti-Sisi movement, they became the central focus of the repressive measures. Within six months, at least 1,000 students had seen their names forcibly removed from the student register and over 1,500 had been arrested. Unknown numbers remain in pre-trial detention – in June 2016, the Interior Ministry announced that some 200 students would be taking their final exams in prison.[21] The powers of the

---

21 Egypt: Years of Abuses Under Al Sisi. www.hrw.org (https://www.hrw.org/news/2015/06/08/egypt-year-abuses-under-al-sisi) 8 June 2015

military courts were significantly expanded. Now they were licensed to prosecute various kinds of 'opinion crime', for instance under the heading of 'sabotaging educational institutions'; such offences were punished with long prison sentences. The media followed suit, spreading the idea of an international conspiracy against Egypt, led by the Muslim Brotherhood and foreign reporters.

The regime's violent quashing of all opposing viewpoints and Sisi's own aggressive moves to consolidate his power in state and society were both attempts to obliterate all signs of the previous revolutionary upheaval. The legal measures taken (in the name of fighting terrorism and re-establishing stability) were unprecedented even by Egyptian standards. The power of the security forces was massively increased, from universities and religious institutions to civil society and the internet. Cleverly worded clauses allowed any criticism of the Sisi regime to be legally construed as treason. An Egyptian 'thought police' is in the making: officially named the 'Municipal Police', its task will be to bring together groups of 'elites' in each residential district, who will then report at regular meetings on any 'suspicious activity' and keep tabs on foreigners in their neighbourhood. The aim: to create a police database of politically suspect citizens.

At the same time, the regime does its best to obstruct the efforts of foreign NGOs working to strengthen democracy and the rule of law. According to article 78 of the criminal code, adopted in September 2014, any Egyptian 'who accepts financial or other support from a foreign country to intentionally commit any act that harms the national interest or jeopardises the independence of the country or its unity or the safety and security of its lands or to commit any acts of hostility against Egypt or to breach public peace and order will be penalised with life imprisonment and a heavy fine.'[22] The fine was set at $70,000, and if the culprit was a state employee, the courts could impose the death penalty rather than life-long imprisonment. Foreign NGOs operate under the ever-present threat of being charged, banned, or having their assets confiscated. As early as June 2013, 43 foreign NGO workers were sentenced by courts dominated by Mubarak loyalists to prison terms of one to five years.

A Human Rights Watch report of 7 November 2014 cited an official figure of 22,000 Egyptian arrests since the coup in July of the previous year, at the same time pointing out that unofficial estimates were sometimes twice as high. The picture hasn't improved since then. Human Rights Watch concluded that Washington, London, Paris and other Western governments had done nothing to prevent the dramatic decline of the human rights situation in the region.

Megalomania as Manifesto

Why would they? Sisi is pro-West. He enjoys the apparently limitless support of the Gulf States. With two billion dollars a year, Egypt is the largest recipient of US financial aid after Israel, and much of that money is used to buy US weapons. After the coup – 'takeover' is the preferred term in Washington and Brussels – the Americans suspended weapons deliveries to Egypt for a few months. But by the time the Gaza War was raging in the summer of 2014, all reservations had been forgotten, and the West was treating him as an invaluable intermediary between

---

22 Reem Gehad. 'Egypt amends penal code to stipulate harsher punishments on foreign funding', Ahram Online, 23 September 2014 (http://english.ahram.org.eg/NewsContent/1/64/111488/Egypt/Politics-/Egypt-amends-penal-code-to-stipulate-harsher-punis.aspx)

Hamas, Israel and themselves, entrusting him to negotiate a ceasefire. Hamas had emerged out of the Palestinian Muslim Brotherhood, and had close ties to Egypt, yet now the man who'd had 1,000 Muslim Brothers shot was acting as an intermediary. Or was it precisely because of this that the West chose him?

Egypt's short-term future is all too easy to guess. More of the Muslim Brotherhood will go underground, joining those who have already done so. Other more radical Islamist groups will declare war on the state. Such groups are already active in central Egypt and along the Libyan border. Sisi will react predictably to every terrorist attack: with more repression, which will then provoke further attacks. Sooner or later the situation will come to a dangerous head, not least for economic reasons. Even a well-meaning and competent government committed to transparency and good leadership would struggle to alleviate the enormous social differences and push through economic reform in the teeth of the country's entrenched kleptocracy. There is no such commitment on the part of Sisi's regime. Policies to support middle-class entrepreneurs and 'microcredit' schemes (small loans to help the millions of informal day-workers escape a life of insecurity) form no part of the government's plans. No attempts are being made to improve the dilapidated education system. Instead, the order of the day is investment in gigantic development projects that benefit mainly the Egyptian upper classes, Saudi sponsors and Gulf investors.

There are plans to construct up to 48 new towns and tourist centres, to widen the Suez Canal, to lay down a high-speed train line, to build one million new homes, and to create new industrial zones. This is little short of megalomania in a country where half the population wakes up every morning unsure whether it will eat that day. If Egypt were a company instead of a state, the liquidator would have been called in long ago. The land is *de facto* bankrupt. In the two years after the coup, it received more than $20 million in financial aid from the Gulf States, foremost among them Saudi Arabia, partly as loan, partly as gift. As mentioned above, Saudi Arabia sees Egypt as the front-line state in the battle against the Muslim Brotherhood, and views its financial support as a long-term investment. If, as seems likely, the regime's economic policies fail to improve the lot of the population as a whole, and the state continues on its repressive course, new and increasingly radical protests are to be expected.

America's friends in the Middle East – Egypt, Saudi Arabia, Kuwait and the United Arab Emirates – form a reactionary political alliance that aims to extinguish any glimmerings of democratic protest on the pretext of combatting terrorism. They are united in their determination to prevent at all costs another Arab Spring. These countries act more and more like deputy sheriffs in the region, whose role is merely to follow their master's orders: for example, by intervening in Libya's inter-tribal war with airstrikes. At America's behest, Egyptian troops were apparently on stand-by for a temporary occupation of eastern Libya in order to block the advance of radical Islamists and prevent further weapons smuggling.

Holy Alliances

This alliance of monarchs and generals recalls the European despots in the 19th century who made such concerted efforts to undo the achievements of the French Revolution. The nations who attended the Congress of Vienna in 1815 shared the aim of abolishing of all liberal movements. The 'Holy Alliance' of Austria, Prussia and Russia had been formed to thwart

Napoleon's imperial ambitions while battling republican ideas in their own countries. For decades after Napoleon's defeat, the alliance acted as a feudal rampart, successfully defeating the European revolutions of 1848–9. But although they left a trail of blood whose effects were felt for generations, these repressive, backwards-looking monarchies could not hold back the tide of history for ever. In the end, they were swept away.

It seems unlikely that today's 'Holy Alliance' between Sisi and the Gulf monarchies can obstruct for long the yearning for democratic change. A combination of demographic pressures, the long-term unsustainability of the oil-revenue-dependent economy, and regional instabilities is forging new realities that even the old feudal guard will be unable to escape. America and Europe have put themselves on the side of the reactionaries by tacitly accepting the coup against the Muslim Brotherhood in the most populated, most culturally influential and historically rich Arab country.

The West presents its support of Sisi as a defence of freedom and liberal values against the Muslim Brotherhood. Yet neither Saudi Arabia nor the Sisi regime, to say the least, have thus far been outstanding defenders of such values. In reality, of course, none of this was ever about values; it was about maintaining a status quo useful to Washington and Europe. Shadi Hamid from the thinktank Brookings Institution put it succinctly:

Washington tends to question whether Islamists' religious commitments can coexist with respect for democracy, pluralism, and women's rights. But what the United States really fears are the kinds of foreign policies such groups might pursue. Unlike the Middle East's pro-Western autocracies, Islamists have a distinctive, albeit vague, conception of an

Arab world that is confident, independent, and willing to project influence beyond its borders.[23]

The spectrum of Islamism is broad, stretching from Islamic State to President Erdogan of Turkey. The Western mind, however, befuddled with Islamophobia, fails to differentiate. Political problems involving Muslims, whether in the Middle East or at home among immigrants, are widely blamed on religion. Especially in Europe (less so in the US), the inter-meshing of religion and politics in the Islamic world is viewed with mistrust. There may be good reasons for this, but the fact is that today's Middle East is a fundamentally more religious place than today's Protestant Europe, and no amount of disapproval will alter this reality. Moreover, Islam alone offers a shared identity on the basis of which opposition movements might grow. The secular movements which arose in the industrial societies of the West are inconceivable in the feudal societies that predominate in the Arab-Islamic world. No protest party or movement that is not rooted in Islam has a chance of gaining power.

Reformation! Enlightenment!

There is a widespread belief in the West that the Islamic world, not having been through a Reformation or an Enlightenment, can therefore not become democratic or modern. The unspoken assumption is that history repeats itself according to immutable natural laws. Yet there is no reason why Europe's experiences should serve as a template for those in other parts of the world. The really indispensable precondition for social progress and

23 Shadi Hamid. *Islamic Exceptionalism: How The Struggle Over Islam Is Reshaping The World.* St Martin's Press, 2016.

plurality is not a European-style Reformation and Enlightenment, but the rule of law. Whether the law is secular or founded in religion is of secondary importance. The West's insistence on its own past as the universal blueprint comes from an inflated sense of its own importance.

For the sake of simplicity, modern Islam may be divided into two broad currents. One comes from Egypt, takes its inspiration from the Muslim Brotherhood, and includes the ruling Turkish party AKP, as well as the Palestinian branch of Hamas. The other current issues from Saudi Wahhabism; its most recent product is Islamic State. Despite the massive harm that Wahhabism has caused, it seldom finds itself in the pillory, unlike the Muslim Brotherhood, whose links with the demonised Hamas guarantee Western opprobrium.

In the 1970s, the Muslim Brotherhood experienced a huge upswing in popularity, owing to its fight against social injustice and castigation of power-hungry tribal elites. In Egypt and Syria, part of the Brotherhood went underground and began to use violent methods, which led to their brutal repression in both countries.

Those who would like to see Wahhabism, al-Qaida or Islamic State weakened might do well to see an alternative in the Muslim Brotherhood. Like all mass movements, its ranks contain the moderate and the pragmatic as well as hard-liners and ideologues. Politically, the movement has trodden a long path from underground activity to the highest government office. Despite regional differences, some highly questionable decisions, and not infrequent examples of incompetence, the Muslim Brotherhood is at its core a pragmatic organisation. Its aim is not to create a rigorous, fanatical theocracy of the Saudi or Iranian stripe. The opposition they faced in Egypt from non-Islamist sectors of the population was less a consequence of their religious views than of their shortcomings as a government.

Today's Islamic societies all face this question: how much Islam do we want, what kind, and where? Do we want Islam in our politics? In our daily lives? The tragedy of the military coup in Egypt is that it cut short this painful but urgently needed exercise in democracy, and re-introduced dictatorship. The Generals answered the question in their own way and triggered a spiral of violence that is still in its beginnings.

Tunisia Reborn

Tunisia, the birthplace of the Arab uprisings in December 2010, took a more constructive path. In October 2011, the Ennahda (Renaissance) party, the Tunisian branch of the Muslim Brotherhood, became the strongest group in the elected constituent assembly, which served as a transition government. Waves of rioting and politically motivated violence followed, mostly at the hands of radical Salafists, and two prominent liberal opposition politicians were murdered in 2013.

Under the leadership of Rashid al-Ghaninouchi (repeatedly accused of not acting decisively against the Salafist threat), Ennahda played a significant role in ratifying a new Tunisian constitution in January 2014. The most progressive in the Arab world, it explicitly invokes the Universal Declaration of Human Rights as one of its pillars, as well as espousing an open and tolerant Islam. The constitution guarantees religious freedom to every citizen. Islamic law (*sharia*) was deliberately not used as a basis for legislation. Instead, the separation of religion and state was guaranteed and the rights of women were strengthened. Partly in reaction to the murder of the two opposition politicians, the popular Salafist practice of *takfir* – declaring someone an infidel, and thereby issuing a blanket licence to kill them – was outlawed.

Ghaninouchi, who co-founded Ennahda in 1981 and spent a long period in exile in London, is a leading Islamic intellectual. In 2012, *Time* magazine named him among the 100 most influential people in the world. *Foreign Policy*, the leading US journal of foreign affairs, also placed him on their list of the 100 most important global thinkers. Time and again, in speeches and publications, Ghaninouchi has broached the question of how Islam, freedom, modernity and democracy can be reconciled.

Even before Ennahda won the election in 2011, Ghaninouchi was clear that winning a political majority would not alone be enough to make the successful transition to democracy. A far wider coalition of the various groups in society would be needed. Such views were very different from those held by Morsi and the Muslim Brotherhood in Egypt, It was Ghaninouchi's willingness to engage widely that made a new political start – including the new constitution – possible. The Ennahda party also showed its flexible approach during its first two elections. In 2011, it placed questions of national and religious identity at the centre of its electoral campaign, whereas in the run-up to the parliamentary elections in 2014, it switched its focus to concrete social and economic questions of more direct relevance to the daily lives of Tunisia's struggling population.

Even so, Ennahda lost the election. The newly-founded centrist party *Nida Tunis* ('Call of Tunisia') became the strongest in parliament, having managed to secure the support of the liberal middle classes. In its ranks former officials of the overthrown pre-2011 government rub shoulders with leading trade unionists, left-wing liberal intellectuals and business people. Whether Nida Tunis really stands for change, or will simply hold the back door open for the old squad to come back, remains to be seen. Unlike the Egyptians, however, the Tunisians seem to have found a way to debate constructively the role of religion in government and society, helped by a well-rooted civil society and a strong trade union movement, as well as a relatively high level of general education. Perhaps most importantly, Tunisia's army is small and weak. It is no 'state within a state', and would be incapable of overthrowing the government, even if the top brass wanted to.

Tunisia is the Arab Spring's only success story – if a qualified one – but the country faces some daunting challenges. The economic situation is precarious. In the south, there are regular skirmishes between security forces and jihadists trickling in from Libya and Algeria. Many of IS's foreign fighters hail from Tunisia. Here things come full circle. The West's first crucial mistake is to give Wahhabism free rein while seeing the Muslim Brotherhood as a threat. The second is to assume that a 'Sunni coalition' between the Gulf States and Turkey would be capable of defeating Islamist extremism. The Gulf monarchs have no credibility beyond their own clientele, and are loathed even by many moderate Sunnis. They are also internally divided. Qatar joined Turkey in supporting the Muslim Brotherhood in Egypt, incurring the wrath of its neighbour, Saudi Arabia, which has tried to punish it with isolation. The belief that the so-called 'moderate' Gulf monarchies will act in consort to defeat radical Islam is sheer delusion. By pursuing this wrong-headed agenda, Washington and Europe risk being drawn into a war between the Gulf States and the Shiites in Iraq and Iran.

IS and other extremist groups cannot be defeated without local ground troops supplied by the regular Syrian army. It alone is capable of countering IS's guerrilla gangs. But for this to happen

Western governments would have to put their differences with Assad to one side, at least temporarily. To fight simultaneously against Damascus and IS is ludicrous. Assad's regime shows no sign of falling, and even if Bashar himself were to be killed in an attack, the old elite would remain intact. It is time for the West finally to shelve regime change as a dead-end strategy, and instead to involve Russia and China as vital global allies in the fight against IS.

Regime Change in Iran?

It is time to examine Iran's role in more detail. In 1993, Clinton's government launched its policy of 'Dual Containment' – that is, containment of both Iraq and Iran. Pro-Israel factions in Washington had a guiding hand in the policy, which at the time had nothing to do with Iran's nuclear ambitions. The issue for Israel was Iran's support of the Hezbollah, whose resistance had forced Israel's formidable army into an unconditional retreat from their occupation of South Lebanon (1982–2000). As early as April 1995, Israel and the American Israel Public Affairs Committee (AIPAC), the largest pro-Israeli lobby group in Washington, began to formulate a strategy under the title 'Comprehensive U. S. Sanctions against Iran: A Plan for Action'.

In their detailed study *The Israel Lobby and U.S. Foreign Policy*[24], American political scientists John Mearsheimer and Stephen Walt argue that the AIPAC is pursuing two geostrategic goals, both with great success: the political and economic isolation of Iran, and the prevention of a Palestinian state. AIPAC is extremely well-connected in the world of American politics,

24 John J. Mearsheimer, Stephen Walt. *The Israel Lobby and U.S. Foreign Policy*. Penguin. June 2008.

especially in Congress, and wields great influence when it comes to distributing the funds raised during election campaigns.

Mearsheimer and Walt conclude that these policies helped to poison the climate between Tehran and Washington, which in turn strengthened the influence of Iranian hard-liners who rejected the country's new, more moderate head of state, the reformist President Chatami (1997–2005). Chatami's efforts to place relations with the US on a stable footing came to nothing. Instead, matters worsened when the Bush administration abandoned dual containment after 9/11 in favour of 'regional transformation' – in other words, regime change in both Iraq and Iran.

After President Bush located Iran on the 'axis of evil' in 2002, a torrent of articles by prominent neo-conservatives made the case for war. Michael Ledeen, an American historian and foreign policy analyst – and a leading hawk voice – wrote in the *National Review*: 'There is no more time for diplomatic "solutions". We will have to deal with the terror masters, here and now.' It was at this time that the first moves were made against Iran's nuclear program, which according to Israel and AIPAC, posed an intolerable threat and demanded a US response. The Bush administration needed little persuasion. It intensified economic sanctions, and threatened military action if Iran did not terminate its nuclear program. At the same time, the Pentagon's war-planners (among them the very same people who had masterminded the invasion of Iraq) were outlining strategies for military intervention in Iran, in close collaboration with Israel. Despite this massive pressure, President Bush resisted the temptation to invade Iran: evidently, the disastrous failure of the war in Iraq meant that a repeat performance was out the question.

In 2005 Mahmoud Ahmadinedjad became President of Iran,

strengthening the case of the hawks in Israel and the US. Here was a hard-liner whose anti-Israel rhetoric seemed to prove that an Iran with nuclear weapons would pose an existential threat to Israel. Yet after making one attempt, Ahmadinedjad suspended his country's efforts to lay down the necessary infrastructure to make an atomic weapon.

Twice, in 2007 and 2011, the 'National Intelligence Estimate' – a yearly summary of the most important findings of 16 US secret intelligence agencies – certified that Tehran was not striving to acquire nuclear weapons (discussed in more detail in my book, *Iran: Der Falsche Krieg*).[25] Nevertheless, the nuclear negotiations with Iran became increasingly tense, intermittently threatening to spill over into war.

Two issues were uppermost on the agenda. Did Iran have the right to acquire enriched uranium? And in any case, was there an effective way to stop them? At first, Britain, France and Germany led the negotiations (taking orders from Washington), with the US, Russia and China joining at a later date. Moscow and Beijing played a rather token role in proceedings (although in fact both stood to benefit economically from Iran's isolation, which would enable them to buy its oil for less).

It is difficult to avoid the conclusion that the nuclear wranglings with Iran were merely a means to the end of bringing the only anti-Western power of any significance between Morocco and Indonesia economically to its knees – and so to spark regime change. In his political autobiography, *The Age of Deception: Nuclear Diplomacy in Treacherous Times*,[26] Mohammed el-Baradei,

---

25 Michael Lüders, *Iran: Der Falsche Krieg* (*Iran: The False War*; German language). C.H. Beck. May 2012.

26 Mohammed el-Baradei. *The Age of Deception: Nuclear Diplomacy in Treacherous Times*. Bloomsbury. June 2012.

the Egyptian general director of the International Atomic Energy Agency (IAEA), describes in detail how a final agreement was almost reached on multiple occasions, only to be repeatedly torpedoed at the last moment by Washington.

Meanwhile, the West ratcheted up the sanctions, citing Iran's nuclear program as justification, or else its support for 'terror organisations' (code for Hezbollah and Hamas). The spiralling sanctions reached their zenith in 2012 with the passing of the 'Iran Threat Reduction and Syria Human Rights Act' which imposed stringent limits on Iran's oil exports to the West, almost halving them within a year (though Russia, China and India quickly stepped in to fill the gap). The real problem for Iran's oil industry is not finding an export market, but finding a way to modernise its dilapidated infrastructure, given the many restrictions in place since 1979, which severely limit, for instance, foreign investment in the sector.

Non-US enterprises in key industries or economic sectors that dare to conduct anything beyond very minor business in Iran have long been barred from the American market. Indeed, many non-US firms stopped dealing with Iran altogether, for fear of reprisals from Washington. At the same time, more than a hundred major American corporations, including Apple and Microsoft, have been granted official exemptions, and are able to trade freely in Iran – a handy advantage over their international competitors.

An End to Sanctions?

Of particular importance has been the exclusion of Iranian banks from international transactions, an unprecedented move in the history of sanction politics. No bank transfers can be made into or out of Iran using the standard SWIFT system. These swinge-ing boycotts, which the US have pressurised the United Nations to adopt and which have been taken up wholesale by the Euro-peans, clearly have a purpose that goes well beyond making Iran toe the line over its atomic program.

In 2011/12, the nuclear conflict with Iran moved into its most dangerous phase. With an eye on the US presidential elections of November 2012, Netanyahu's Israeli government and the pro-Is-rael lobby in Washington went all-out to push the administra-tion into a war with Iran, which, they claimed, was on the brink of gathering enough uranium to build an atom bomb.

The Obama administration, however, committed to winding down operations in Iraq and Afghanistan, was loath to consid-er a fresh intervention that might set the whole Middle East aflame. (Even so, much use was made of the empty phrase, 'all options are on the table'.) Netanyahu hinted that Israel could bomb Iran's nuclear sites on its own at any time – knowing very well that if this happened, Obama would face huge pressure to act in support of his country's long-standing ally.

It was only in September 2012 that the danger seemed to have passed, when, after months of strife, Washington stated unequivocally that it would not stand by Israel if it moved against Iran. Within Israel's own security agencies, too, there had been mounting unease at the unforeseeable consequences of an attack. As reward for its restraint, Tel Aviv received billions of dollars in donations, as well as the newest weapons systems, among them the cutting-edge anti-missile package, 'Iron Dome'.

Obama's re-election and the appointment of the reformer Hassan Rouhani as Iranian President the following year led to fresh negotiations. Now the Iranians were not alone in wanting to bring an end to the tensions and the sanctions. The dramatically altered situation in the region, with the rise of Islamic State, meant that the Americans were also eager to find a solution. Obama was more ready than any of his predecessors since Jimmy Carter to strike a deal and come to terms with Iran as a regional power. But he still had to take account of the powerful pro-Israel lobby and the hard-liners in his own country. Many Republicans in particular still supported military action against Iran.

After twelve years of negotiations, the breakthrough came in Vienna on 14 July 2015, when the five nations on the UN Security Council plus Germany agreed a nuclear deal with Tehran. The document, more than 100 pages long and with five appendices, submitted Iran's civil nuclear program to up to 25 years of wide-ranging restrictions and controls. Its aim was to stop Tehran from acquiring fissile material for nuclear weapons, either by enriching uranium to 90 percent or by producing plutonium. The economic sanctions and the weapons embargo were to be lifted in stages, starting in 2016. However, the agreement still had to go through the US parliament, and with Congress thoroughly pro-Israel, and the Republicans holding a majority in both the Senate and the House of Representatives, it came down to a power struggle with Obama. The President emerged narrowly victorious, though it remains to be seen whether his successor will follow through on his campaign promise to scrap the deal.

The best-case scenario is that the nuclear deal will help weaken radical forces within the country and set Iran on the path of liberalisation. In the long term, the lifting of sanctions should provide an economic boost, and may lead to Iran at last becoming securely established as a regional power. It is for this very reason that Saudi Arabia and Israel have rejected the deal – the latter especially does not want its leading position in the Middle East challenged.

Needless to say, the long-standing Western bias towards Israel has had consequences that reach far beyond the nuclear conflict with Iran. Crucially, it has stood in the way of a solution to the Palestinian question, on which America and Europe persist in their largely uncritical support of Israel. The fate of the Palestinians is a key factor in the hostility and resentment towards the West felt by so many in the Middle East. It is not hard to see why. Nowhere does the West's claim to be on the side of freedom, democracy and human rights look more shallow and hypocritical than in the context of Israel and Palestine.

FREE PASS FOR ISRAEL?
THE 2014 ISRAEL-GAZA CONFLICT

The conflict between Israel and Palestine is, among much else, a battle for the moral high ground. In the West – and especially in Germany – Israel is historically seen as the only democracy in the Middle East, under constant threat from the surrounding forces of fanaticism and violence. But more and more cracks are appearing in this narrative. During the 50-day Gaza war, around 2,200 Palestinians, mostly civilians and including almost 500 children, were killed in July and August 2014 alone. On the Israeli side, 71 people died, including six civilians. These numbers speak for themselves – although, of course, every death is one too many. Nevertheless, German leader Angela Merkel was quick to deliver her verdict: Israel was legitimately defending itself against the terror of Hamas. It was, almost word-for-word, how she had justified the Gaza conflicts of 2008–09 and of 2012, as well as Israel's invasion of Lebanon in 2006 (with the only difference that the culprit cited in the last case was Hezbollah rather than Hamas).

Since April 2006, the Israeli army has killed more than 7,500 Lebanese and Palestinian people, most of them civilians, yet Western governments persist in viewing its operations as legitimate self-defence. Neither in Berlin nor Brussels, let alone in Washington, has the notion that Israel should be held to the norms of international law gained serious support. No Israeli government since 1967 has had to fear more than the occasional appeal for 'restraint', and gentle hints that Israel's aggressive settlement policy may not be conducive to peace. The systematic stripping of rights from Palestinians in the territories occupied since the Six Day War in 1967, the ongoing occupation of their land, the appalling living conditions in the Gaza Strip – these are all readily observable facts. Yet Western politicians cling to the fiction of a 'peace process' that in truth is a mere facade behind which Tel Aviv can build yet more settlements and create yet more depressing statistics. Under international law, the Gaza Strip is still classified as occupied territory, despite the Israeli withdrawal in 2005, because Israel controls all of its entrances by air, sea and road – even, in cooperation with Egypt, its access via Rafah to Sinai. The UN has stated that by 2020 the Gaza Strip will simply no longer be habitable for the 1.8 million people who will live there.

If people of the Jewish faith anywhere in the world lived under similar conditions to the Palestinians under Israeli occupation, or had to face what inhabitants of the Gaza Strip endured in the summer of 2014, there would be an outcry among Western governments and in the media. Yet the Western line, endlessly repeated, is that Hamas first provoked the war, then rejected a truce. This is wide of the mark, to say the least, but it is still accepted by the majority, though public scepticism vis-à-vis the official version seems to be growing.

Guilt and Atonement

The bias of the West towards Israel has consequences. It makes a mockery of its endlessly repeated commitment to democracy and human rights, which many in the Middle East view as mere synonyms for hypocrisy and double-standards. It weakens the position of moderate Arabs; it strengthens Islamist movements; and it contributes to radicalisation on the street, not least among Muslim immigrants in the West.

Many Europeans find it difficult to grasp the strength of feeling that Israel's treatment of the Palestinian people provokes outside the Western hemisphere. German politicians tend to justify their uncritical attitude with terms like 'reasons of state' or 'special historical responsibility', yet there has been no public debate about what is actually meant by these mantra-like phrases. The collective sense of guilt over the Holocaust has engendered an unquestioning and excessive loyalty to Israel: this is seen as *the* lesson of German history. If politicians or journalists do hazard a word or two of criticism, they keep it superficial, taking refuge in vague common-places about the 'human tragedies': citing, for instance, the 'irreconcilable hatred' on both sides (Israeli as well as Palestinian), or an 'unsolvable conflict', if not a 'biblical' one. The result is that the actual core of the issue remains unnamed. The deliberate, systematic expulsion of around half the Palestinian population during the founding of the state of Israel hardly gets a mention, and the same goes for the continuing settlement of the Palestinian territories conquered in 1967.

This is no conflict among equals. Israel is one of the strongest military powers in the world, and by far the strongest in the Middle East. Although it is a nuclear power, it is not obliged to submit its arsenal to international control (unlike Iran). Yet for the most part the West continues to see Israel as locked in a battle for its very survival, under threat from Palestinians, other Arab states, Iran... Hamas is viewed as the incarnation of fanaticism and terror. The growing right-wing extremism of Israeli society, and the widespread, violent hatred of Arabs, is reported objectively by the media, but its implications are rarely explored. For the majority, Islam alone epitomises violence, and the actions of Hamas provide the proof (if proof were needed). In this climate, nuanced analysis is regarded as little different from condoning terrorism. The possibility that there could be such a thing as an Israeli – let alone a Jewish – brand of fanaticism is not admitted. Unignorable instances of such fanaticism are written off as individual aberrations within an otherwise spotless democracy.

Are we allowed to criticise Israel? In Germany, where any such criticism is apt to be decried as a new outbreak of anti-Semitism, the question invariably arises whenever public opinion threatens to swing in favour of the Palestinians – as it almost did during the last Gaza conflict, when the violence of the Israeli state became all too visible. There were demonstrations all over Germany, and images were broadcast across the media of Palestinians displaying hate-filled slogans. These were deemed proof of anti-Semitism, rather than, say, of rage or frustration. The Israeli ambassador complained of an unprecedented rise in hostility towards Jews. German politicians of all stripes joined the clamour, and promised to do everything they could to fight anti-Semitism, uttering not a word of sympathy for the suffering people of Gaza, let alone any criticism of Israel. By September, just after the end of the war, normality seemed to have returned, as thousands of Germans gathered at the Brandenburg Gate to hear a string of state dignitaries castigate anti-Semitism. Once again, the approximately 2,200 dead people in Gaza were not mentioned.

Let us try to clarify precisely what 'anti-Semitism' means. Take a Palestinian whose parents or grandparents were driven from their homes in 1948, who himself fled to Germany from Lebanon in the 1980s, who perhaps has relatives in Gaza. If this man publicly yells out his rage at Israel, should he be put in the same box as Joseph Goebbels? Is violence against Israelis a more heinous crime than violence against Palestinians? Is stoking anti-Jewish sentiment worse than agitating against Arabs and Muslims? What exactly is the problem with condemning the wrongdoing of both sides equally? Why not call both Palestinian terrorism and Israeli state violence (state *terrorism*?) by their name? Are ethical norms and international laws universally applicable? Or must Palestinians simply accept that Israel gets a free pass, because of what was done to the Jews by others – by the Germans – in the death factories of Nazi Europe?

A New Round of 'Peace Processes'

Germany's uncritical attitude to Israel is a blend of cowardice and hypocrisy. Friends – or allies, if that is what Germany and Israel are – owe each other honesty, including honest criticism. Is it really impossible for Germans to denounce anti-Semitism and acknowledge their nation's guilt for the Holocaust, yet at the same time voice criticism of Israel when it flagrantly violates international law? Even within Israel, leaders of NGOs and what is left of the peace movement regularly call upon international actors, especially Germany, to speak out. Israel is on track to become an ethnocracy, with the Jewish minority holding sway over the non-Jewish majority between the Mediterranean and the Jordan River. The conflict between Israelis and Palestinians is inexorably broadening from a dispute about nationhood into a religious war between Jews and Muslims. There are many ways for Israel to commit suicide, and this is one of them.

For nine months, the US Secretary of State John Kerry tried to resuscitate the 'Peace Process' between Israel and Palestine. In March 2014, he admitted defeat, implying that the intransigence of the Israeli government was to blame. Meanwhile Netanyahu's people counter-briefed journalists that Kerry had deliberately allowed the talks to founder. In April, Fatah and Hamas, the two largest – and hitherto deeply divided – Palestinian organisations, signed a conciliation agreement, and formed a government of national unity made up of moderate technocrats without a single Hamas member. Both Brussels and Washington welcomed this development. Netanyahu, on the other hand, responded with a vicious attack on Mahmoud Abbas, leader of Fatah and president of the Palestinian National Authority, claiming that there was 'no difference' between him and the terrorists. Israel then blocked the transfer of wages for 43,000 Hamas officials in the Gaza Strip.

When three Israeli teenagers were kidnapped in the West Bank on 12 June, Netanyahu immediately and publicly blamed the Hamas leadership, who strongly denied any involvement. Netanyahu insisted he had unambiguous evidence that Hamas was behind the kidnapping, though he never provided this evidence. Later it transpired that the kidnapper had belonged to a clan sympathetic to Hamas, but that he had probably been acting on his own initiative. Netanyahu continued to exploit the affair to discredit the conciliatory policies of the new Palestinian unity government. Murders of this sort, he declared, were the inevitable consequence of an 'alliance' with Hamas.

Although the Israeli police ascertained very soon after the kidnapping that the three teenagers had already been killed, they withheld this information until 1 July. In the meantime, on Netanyahu's orders, the army assaulted political organisations and welfare institutions in the West Bank, and arrested hundreds of Hamas members. A wave of anti-Arab hatred washed over Israel and the settlements. Among the victims was a 16-year-old Palestinian boy, Mohammed Abu Kheir, who was burnt alive in east

Jerusalem. Israeli attacks on the Gaza Strip began on 12 June. Initially Hamas did not return fire, though other more radical organisations like Islamic Jihad did. It was not until 7 July that Hamas first retaliated, after Israeli bombs had killed six of its operatives in Gaza the previous night. With this, the truce that had concluded the last war between Israel and Hamas in 2012, came to an end.

It is worth repeating that between November 2012 and July 2014, Hamas *did not fire a single rocket* at Israel. Despite its close ties with the army, the Israeli thinktank 'Meir Amit Intelligence and Terrorism Information Center' acknowledged as much in its weekly bulletin of 2–8 July 2014: 'For the first time since Operation Pillar of Defence [November 2012], Hamas participated in and claimed responsibility for rocket fire.' Even the pro-Netanyahu *Jerusalem Post* had reported in May 2013 that Hamas was acting to *thwart* rocket attacks from Gaza.[27] In the West, though, the roles of 'good guys' and 'bad guys' showed no signs of being re-allocated. On 23 July, beneath the headline 'Hamas Gambled on War as Its Woes Grew in Gaza', the *New York Times* reported that 'when Hamas sent a barrage of rockets into Israel, simmering hostilities and back-and-forth strikes erupted into war.'

Hamas 'Does Not Recognise Israel'?

To recap: Netanyahu's government allowed the American-led 'Peace Process' to fail, then it used the murder of three Israeli teenagers as the pretext to start a war with Gaza whose main aim was to torpedo the Unity Government once and for all. Yet it was not the Israeli government that ended up the dock, but

---

27 'IDF Source: Hamas Working To Stop Gaza Rockets'. *Jerusalem Post*, May 3 2013

Hamas, as long-honed Western reflexes kicked in. These reflexes were, however, out-of-date. It is true that the Hamas Charter of 1988 had listed the 'destruction of Israel' among its goals, but in the eight years since their electoral victory the party had changed, like every party that makes the transition from opposition to government.

Israel and the West had responded to Hamas's victory in 2006 by doing everything possible to prevent the party from taking over the Palestinian National Authority. With the connivance of Mahmoud Abbas, the Fatah leader, who had an axe to grind after his election defeat, heavy fighting broke out between Fatah and Hamas, which led to the Palestinian territories being split in two. Since then, Hamas has controlled the Gaza Strip while the National Authority, dominated by Fatah, controls the West Bank. There have been no parliamentary elections since 2006, owing to the high probability of another Hamas victory.

When asked by the *Washington Post* in February 2006 if Hamas was ready to recognize the state of Israel, its leader Ismail Haniyeh, Prime Minister of Palestine from 2006 to 2007, replied: 'Let Israel recognize the legitimate rights of the Palestinians first, and then we will have a position regarding this.'[28] In March 2006, Hamas published a new political program which, unlike the 1988 Charter, made no reference to the 'historical Palestine'. In June of the same year, Haniyeh dictated a letter, which was eventually delivered via intermediaries to President Bush. It said: 'We are so concerned about stability and security in the area that we don't mind having a Palestinian state within the 1967 borders and offering a truce for many years.' Haniyeh went on to urge the US to lift its boycott: 'the continuation of

28 Lally Weymouth. 'A Conversation With Ismail Haniyeh'. *Washington Post*. 26 February 2006.

this situation,' he wrote, 'will encourage violence and chaos in the whole region.'[29]

Bush's government did not see fit to answer Haniyeh's letter, and Israel continued as before. In 2006 alone, 660 Palestinians were killed in Gaza by Israeli bombs and rockets, most of them civilians, a third of them children. The UN estimated the number of Palestinians killed by Israel between April 2006 and July 2012 at 2,879. Up to the start of the 2014 war, rockets launched from Gaza had killed a total of 28 Israelis. After Hamas's election victory in 2006, the European Union followed Washington's lead in putting the party on the terror list, citing their historic pledge to 'destroy' Israel. At the same time, Israel introduced drastic controls on traffic of goods into Gaza, including food and medicine.

'The way to think of it is as a kind of diet,' suggested Dov Weisglass, an influential advisor to the then Prime Minister, Ariel Sharon. 'We are causing [the Palestinians] to become thinner, but not so thin that they die.' Notwithstanding these tender scruples, food imports fell below what was needed to ensure the daily minimum of necessary calories: with the official rate of unemployment at 50 percent, four fifths of Gaza's population are dependent on UN food aid. (Incidentally, about the same proportion – 80% – are refugees, or are descended from refugees who fled Israel in 1947/48 or were expelled from the West Bank in 1967.)

According to aid workers, it was not long after the introduction of the 'diet' before children in particular began to show signs of malnourishment and anaemia, or became ill with typhoid and diarrhoea. The embargo was an indiscriminate and collective punishment, with no attempt made to spare the vulnerable or

---

29 Barak Ravid/Haaretz Correspondent. 'In 2006 Letter to Bush, Haniyeh Offered Compromise With Israel'. 14 November 2008.

innocent. The Israeli historian and Oxford Professor of International Relations, Avi Shlaim, put it like this:

> America and the EU shamelessly joined Israel in ostracising and demonising the Hamas government and in trying to bring it down by withholding tax revenues and foreign aid. A surreal situation thus developed with a significant part of the international community imposing economic sanctions, not against the occupier but against the occupied, not against the oppressor but against the oppressed. As so often in the tragic history of Palestine, the victims were blamed for their own misfortunes.[30]

Israel was left free to continue its attacks on the Gaza Strip, while Hamas was ordered to cease fire. Despite the international boycott of the Hamas government, it was supposed to behave as the West's deputy sheriff, policing its militants, stopping the rockets. Meanwhile, the food shortage led to the mass building of tunnels from Gaza into Sinai: until the 2013 Egyptian coup, most supplies were delivered via this route. The tunnels were also used to smuggle in weapons, and in the New Year of 2008/9 Israel launched 'Operation Cast Lead' – three weeks of ground invasions and bombardments during which 1,400 Palestinians were killed.

'Lawn Mowing'

Do the Israeli government and its friends in the West really believe that people living under conditions of daily bombardment and slow starvation will simply roll over, offering no resistance?

30 Avi Shlaim. 'How Israel Brought Gaza To The Brink Of Humanitarian Catastrophe'. *Guardian*, 7 Jan 2009

It goes without saying that the people of Israel have a right to live in freedom and security, and to defend themselves. Whether the regular attacks on Gaza ('lawn mowing' as officials like to call them) help to create such conditions is another matter.

Hamas *must recognise Israel and renounce violence*. This has become an article of faith, endlessly repeated by politicians and in the media, both in Israel and the West. Everything else is secondary: the suffering in Gaza, the real complexities of the situation. It is striking how seldom one hears the inverse demand: that Israel define the borders within which it wishes to be recognised. Alone among UN member states, Israel has never formally declared where its borders are. It is also worth making the point that the Palestine Liberation Organisation (PLO) and Fatah both officially recognised Israel in 1988. Did it make a difference? It is hard to think so: Israeli settlement continued unabated, and peace remained elusive.

By the end of the 1930s, the Palestinians had already lost the battle against Zionism. Even if they were to be given their own state in the territories occupied by Israel since 1967, it would be less than a quarter of the size of their old homeland. Of course, no Israeli government has been prepared to cede even this, despite agreeing to do so in the 1993 Oslo Accords. Despite this, the West regularly appeals to the Palestinians to show themselves 'willing to compromise' and to rein in their demands, while Israel, which is pursuing an illegal settlement policy, is let off the hook. For the Palestinians it is a lose-lose situation: if they are moderate, they get nothing; if they use violence, they are labelled as terrorists, and get nothing. If Israel uses violence, then it's self-defence.

Why is the Israeli government so against a Palestinian state? The real cause has less to do with power politics and more with ideology. Israel's ultra-nationalists have enjoyed an alarming surge in popularity since Prime Minister Yitzhak Rabin was murdered in 1995 by a Jewish right-wing extremist: they won clear majorities in the parliamentary elections of both 2013 and 2015. They regard all the territory between the Mediterranean and the Jordan River as their biblically Promised Land; and the West Bank, corresponding to the ancient Jewish regions of Judea and Samaria, is part of it. To them, the idea of handing this God-given territory to anyone else is patently absurd.

In this scheme, the 'Palestinians' do not exist. They are an invented people, a false category, an anomalous terror in their midst. The most radical Israeli settlers would have all Arabs expelled into Sinai, Lebanon or Jordan. So far this has not happened, but what the Palestinians have to endure within Israel, exposed to policies that make their daily lives hell and take away their livelihoods (especially those of farmers), is not so much better. And all the time the hope of the occupiers, by no means always unspoken, that one day they will simply give up and leave their homeland. Those who actually do this lose their right to live in the West Bank or eastern Jerusalem after seven years. The same, of course, does not apply to Israelis, who are free to emigrate to New York or Berlin and return whenever they like.

Back to the Gaza War. On 8 July 2014, Israel officially launched 'Operation Protective Edge'. Its military objectives were hazy: Netanyahu spoke of 'restoring calm' in the south of Israel; the Minister of Defence, Moshe Ya'lon, cited 'no rockets' as the goal; later, Netanyahu expressed a wish to make Hamas pay 'a heavy price'.

On 15 July, the Israeli cabinet agreed to a truce suggested by Egypt, based on the terms of the ceasefire of 2012. Hamas refused, since their demands that the blockade be lifted and the borders reopened were not part of the deal. When, shortly afterwards, Hamas fighters succeeded in getting onto Israeli soil through a tunnel, the government ordered the total destruction of all tunnels, for the first time since the hostilities began. This marked the start of the ground offensive, which wreaked devastating destruction and caused huge loss of life.

The Middle East's longest war to date ended on 26 August with a truce of 'unlimited duration' mediated by Egypt. The details were not made public, on the grounds that further negotiations were planned to secure a permanent ceasefire. At the time of writing, these have not yet taken place. It is clear that no long-term solution in Gaza is possible unless the blockade is lifted; all Palestinian factions are united in making this demand. Yet, apart from the odd symbolic gesture on the part of Israel, there is nothing to suggest this will happen. As long as there is no Palestinian state, the Gaza Strip will remain trapped in political limbo. The next armed conflict can only be a matter of time.

Destruction 'Beyond Description'

Notwithstanding the high Palestinian body count and the widespread destruction of Gaza in 2014, Israel achieved no victory worthy of the name. Contrary to the official version of events, this war was not about tunnels. Neither was it about rockets. It was about re-establishing the status quo, destroying the Palestinian Unity Government, and returning the 'peace process' to its proper place as a purely decorative entity.

For many Israelis – and for their ultra-nationalist governments – Hamas represents the incarnation of pure evil (along with Iran). It follows that reconciliation between Hamas and Fatah must be prevented at all costs. The Israeli government's ideal situation would be for a weakened Mahmoud Abbas to serve as front for a nominal 'peace process' (rather than the much-needed powerful advocate for real change), while Israel goes full steam ahead with ever more massive construction plans in the West Bank and eastern Jerusalem.

During a visit in October 2014, UN Secretary-General Ban Ki-Moon characterised the destruction of the Gaza Strip as 'beyond description'. The war had seen around 2,200 dead and more than 10,000 injured. Whole districts flattened; 175 factories destroyed. Huge mountains of ruins; four million tons of rubble, with no means of disposal. No machinery to rebuild; nothing to export even if export markets could be reached; no more space for rubbish tips. Sewage treatment plants either destroyed or non-existent; raw sewage running into the open sea; the ground-water polluted and salinated; the soil becoming steadily infertile. Not enough electricity supply for more than a few hours a day; most of the power lines down in any case. The health service in tatters; almost all schools in ruins or in use as emergency shelters.

According to Sara Roy of the Centre for Middle Eastern Studies at Harvard, 450,000 inhabitants of Gaza have no access to clean drinking water and at least 370,000 are seriously traumatised.[31] The destruction of the factories has cost thousands of jobs. Tens of thousands of people live in ruins, with about 17,000 homes reduced to rubble. Almost all UN-built facilities lie in ruins or have been heavily damaged. The Israel-Gaza conflict of 2014 finally broke the back of the economy and all but wiped out the middle class. Only poverty unites this fractured society now.

The Palestinian National Authority puts the cost of reconstruction at $7.8 billion, though Sara Roy doubts the

---

31 Bettina Marx. 'The Back of the Gazan Economy has been Broken.' www.en.qantara.de. 7 October 2014.

very possibility of 'rebuilding' the Gaza Strip. 'What should be rebuilt?' she asks. 'Only the destruction from 2014, or do we include the damage resulting from the military operations of 2000, 2003, 2005, 2006, and so on?' The devastation of 2014 hit a Gaza Strip that was already hollowed out, a society economically and emotionally on the verge of collapse. Roy's view is that Israel will not for much longer get away with its repeated attacks on the infrastructure, while the rest of the world pays for the reconstruction.

On this last point, Roy may well be mistaken. In October 2014, the first 'pledging conference' was held in Cairo; nobody suggested that Israel should contribute. Since the 1993 Oslo Accords, the EU has invested €100 million in Gaza's infrastructure, including in a new airport. It has all been destroyed – the justification, as ever, being that Hamas was using it for terrorism. No bill has been sent to Israel; nor have 'red lines' been drawn that are not to be crossed in the future. In 2000, Israel and the EU managed to conclude an 'association agreement', whose 154 pages included not one instance of the word 'Palestine' nor any reference to the Israeli occupation. Instead, at Israel's instigation, the agreement declared: 'The EU is committed to continuing its ongoing fruitful cooperation with Israel as regards the fight against xenophobia, discrimination and anti-Semitism.'[32]

War Crimes? What War Crimes?

In July 2014, Israel's actions in Gaza prompted six Nobel Peace Prize winners, hundreds of intellectuals from all over the world,

---

[32] EU-Israel Association Agreement. Signed 20 November 1995. Entered into force 1 June 2000. (http://eeas.europa.eu/archives/delegations/israel/eu_israel/political_relations/agreements/index_en.htm)

dozens of churches across the US, and several Jewish organisations to write an open letter demanding the immediate cessation of all military cooperation with the Jewish state.[33]

The German government, meanwhile, was moving in the opposite direction. In October of that year, it made the decision to sell two corvette gun-boats to Tel Aviv. These usually cost €1 billion, but Germany's 'special historical responsibility' towards Israel meant that Berlin offered a discount of €300 million of taxpayers' money. If we factor in a string of special deals linked to the sale of a total of eight submarines to Israel since 2000, the German taxpayer has subsidised the Israeli military to the tune of just under €2 billion – this despite the fact that officially Berlin does not sell any weapons into war zones.

It is highly probable that these German boats will be used in the next Gaza War to bombard strips of coastline. Here, then, is the lesson German politicians have drawn from their country's history: that they have a duty to sell Israel weapons at mates' rates, so that they can then be used for killing Palestinians.

In July 2014, the UN Human Rights Council launched a commission to investigate possible war crimes by both the Israelis and Palestinians. Israel refused to allow the commission into the country, citing its hostility towards the Jewish state. It is not hard to imagine what would have happened if Tehran had used a similar argument to block the International Atomic Energy Authority from visiting their nuclear facilities.

At first, the commission was led by Canadian lawyer William Schabas, whom the Israeli foreign secretary accused of being 'prejudiced' because he repeatedly criticised occupation policies. Schabas was forced to step down and was replaced by US lawyer

33 Desmond Tutu, et al. 'The Arms Trade And Israel's Attack On Gaza.' 8 July 2014. *Guardian*.

Mary McGowan Davis, who was more sympathetic to Israel's position. In June 2015, the UNHRC published its report. It documented the suffering caused to the Israeli civilian population by the rocket bombardment from Gaza. (Thousands of rockets were indeed fired, though most were intercepted by the 'Iron Dome' defence system.) Since these rockets were aimed at Israeli cities, threatening mostly civilians, they could be counted as a Palestinian war crime, perpetrated against Israel.

Nevertheless, the centrepiece of the report was a detailed exposition of Israel's 'violations of international law'. Prime Minister Netanyahu dismissed it as nothing but a 'rape of the truth', and the liberal newspaper *Haaretz* predicted that the report would only 'embed Israelis ever deeper in their isolated bunkers', and that the diplomatic offensive launched by the government against its findings would turn out to be a prelude to further repression of the Palestinian people.

The first casualty of war is the truth, as the saying goes. One of the greatest lies in the Gaza War was the claim that Israel tried to protect civilians. With the help of diagrams, the Israeli human rights organisation *B'Tselem* has shown how whole families were eliminated in indiscriminate carpet bombings. The blog *+972 Magazine* – which along with *Haaretz* represents the last bastion of the liberal media in Israel – points out that there is no evidence that Hamas used people as human shields, prevented civilians from fleeing, or forced them to stay inside their homes or on their roofs. The Israeli army, on the other hand, repeatedly used Palestinian students as human shields, carried out summary executions, and looted the houses they searched. As in previous Gaza wars, UN establishments were attacked, including schools filled with refugees. The worst incident occurred on 2 August in Rafah, when 30 people seeking shelter were killed by a single bomb. The UN Secretary General called it a 'criminal act'. The Israeli response was the standard one: that the schools concealed weapons stashes, or served as launch stations for rockets.

'Killing Snakes'

The Gaza Strip is about the size of the metropolitan area of Glasgow or the German city of Bremen. About half of this region is built on; the rest is semi-desert. All border crossings are closed. There is not one air raid shelter. Any attack on such a territory is an attack on the civilian population; destruction of vital infrastructure is inevitable. The point of the Gaza War was to send a message to the Palestinians that they had no chance. That they would never get their state, that all resistance was futile, that they should accept defeat. Israeli politicians make no secret of this attitude. At the beginning of the offensive, the Deputy Speaker in the Knesset, Likud's Moshe Feiglin, proposed giving the 'enemy population' a single ultimatum to flee to Sinai. 'This will be the limit of Israel's humanitarian efforts,' he said, suggesting that it should be followed by carpet bombing 'without consideration for "human shields" or "environmental damage"'.[34] On her Facebook page, Knesset delegate Ayelet Shaked, Netanyahu's chief administrator from 2006 to 2008 and Justice Minister since 2015, posted an article recommending the killing of Palestinian mothers who might bear 'little snakes'. The Palestinian people, according to her post, consisted of 'enemy combatants, and their blood shall be on all their heads. Now this also includes the mothers of the martyrs, who send them to hell with flowers and kisses. They should follow their sons, nothing would be more

oshe Feiglin. 'My Gaza Solution'. *Jewish Press*. 23 July 2014.

just. They should go, as should the physical homes in which they raised the snakes. Otherwise, more little snakes will be raised there.'[35]

Before it was taken down, the post attracted thousands of 'likes', and reflected a fundamental mood that settled upon the Israeli media in general. With a few exceptions, the message was the same everywhere: the use violence was warmly endorsed, while readers were spared any description or images of the human misery inflicted on Gaza. The human rights group *B'Tselem* tried to book an advertising slot on national radio to read out the names of Palestinian civilians who had been killed. Ordinary radio coverage of the Palestinian death toll was unthinkable. *B'Tselem's* request was legally blocked. Never before had the people of Israel, or more precisely the Jewish people of Israel, been so unanimously in support of the government as during the Israel-Gaza conflict of 2014. Decades of occupation and the accompanying dehumanisation of the Palestinians had done their work. Anyone who has watched how young Israeli reservists, barely out of school, treat Palestinians at the Qalandia border crossing, has seen what racism truly looks like.

Political debate in Israel is no longer between conservatives, liberals and social democrats, nor even between pro-peace and pro-settlement movements, but between three ultra-nationalist parties. The largest, *Likud*, is led by Netanyahu; the second biggest – *Ha-Beit Ha-Yihudi* or *The Jewish Home* – by the current Minister of Education, Naftali Bennett; and the third – *Yisrael Beiteinu* or *Our Home, Israel* – by Avigdor Lieberman, who was foreign minister until 2015. These parties scarcely differ in

35 Gideon Resnick. 'Israeli Politician Declares War On The Palestinian People'. www.dailybeast.com. 7 August 2014. (http://www.thedailybeast.com/articles/2014/07/07/israeli-politician-declares-war-on-the-palestinian-people.html)

message; they merely target different sections of the electorate. None have the slightest intention of making peace with the Palestinians.

Since the 2014 Gaza conflict, racism in Israel has completely lost its inhibitions. Young Israelis post photos on Facebook with slogans like 'Hating Arabs is not racism, it's a value system.' The Foreign Minister at the time recommended taking citizenship away from Palestinians with Israeli passports. A fifth of all Israeli citizens are Palestinians, most living in Galilee. To the majority of the population, though, they are neither Israelis nor Palestinians; they are simply Arabs. They have never been anything other than second-class citizens. Thus Palestinian town councils receive less than half the budget of Jewish communities. Palestinians are not allowed to do certain jobs, and are seldom and only with great difficulty able to secure bank loans. Avigdor Lieberman has suggested giving the Israeli Palestinians money to 'disappear'. Shimon Gafsou, mayor of the uptown, Jewish district of Nazareth (the inner city is majority Palestinian) has demanded that the town's Arab population be kept in check. Israeli politicians advocate boycotting Palestinian businesses. The first 'Palestinans-only' bus lines have been introduced. A theme park in Rishon LeZion has a separate access for Jews and Arabs. Palestinians are often not served in restaurants. More and more companies will only hire Jews .

Correspondingly, outbreaks of violence have also significantly increased. Attacks on Palestinian establishments, houses or mosques have become regular occurrences in Israel and on the West Bank. In the Israeli media, these events are condoned as 'price tag attacks' – meaning that they are intended to extract a price from anyone opposed to Jewish settlement. In November 2014, the 'Max Rayne Hand in Hand Jerusalem School', the largest Jewish-Arab institution in the country (it offers bilingual lessons in Hebrew and Arabic) fell victim to an arson attack. Slogans like 'There's no co-existence with cancer' and 'Death to Arabs' were sprayed on the school walls. On the other side, the mounting hatred and frustration of Palestinians has led to more and more acts of violence committed by individuals: one such attack on a synagogue, also in November 2014, killed four people.

It is not only Arabs who are made to feel the collective hatred and rejection of Israel's Jewish population. It's also Israeli soldiers who dare to voice criticism of army, as well as members of the peace movement or just Israelis of liberal persuasion who condemn violence and prejudice. Gideon Levy, one of the sharpest critics of Israeli occupation policy and a columnist for *Haaretz,* received multiple death threats during the most recent Gaza War. Since then, he has not appeared in public without bodyguards.

The Path to Apartheid

The climate of opinion in Israel has much to do with the refusal on the part of Israeli society and the Jewish diaspora to look clearly and critically at their own history. Inconvenient truths are suppressed, and victims recast as enemies, on the wrong side of history in every sense of the word. Until the 1930s there were two main currents of thought within the Zionist movement. One group, admittedly the smaller one, wanted to build a Jewish state together with the Palestinians (among their best-known advocates was the philosopher, Martin Buber). The majority, though, were in favour of the 'conquest of land' and the 'conquest of labour' – in other words, resettling the Palestinians and taking their jobs.

After the founding of the State of Israel in 1948, these so-called 'Revisionists', the ancestors of today's ultra-nationalist right, played a leading role in clearing about 800,000 Palestinians – almost half of the population – from their homeland. Massacres were a deliberate part of this operation.

This 'original sin' remains a taboo subject, and even today very few Israeli historians broach it. As a result, very few ordinary Israelis know, for instance, that Palestinians residing in urban areas such as Jaffa were forced until the 1950s to live in specific districts, under heavy guard and surrounded with barbed wire. If they wanted to leave, they had to apply for an official permit.

When the PLO formed in 1965, Prime Minister Golda Meir claimed there was no such thing as 'Palestinians' and never had been. Shorly after signing the Oslo Accords in 1993, which were supposed to lay the foundations for a Palestinian state, Israel launched the biggest building program in the West Bank since the start of the occupation in 1967. This was despite Prime Minister Yitzhak Rabin's public support for peace. Like many Israelis, he too was internally conflicted. Peace, yes, but at what price?

In 2000, Ariel Sharon gave his own answer to this question when he made his fateful visit to the Temple Mount, thereby triggering the second *intifada*. Sharon declared the Oslo Accords 'dead' and abruptly cut off Israeli negotiations with the Palestinians, calling Yasser Arafat a terrorist, isolating his government and shelling its headquarters in Ramallah to rubble. The result was to strengthen Hamas (the group had emerged during the first intifada of 1987, ironically with the support of Israel, which at the time viewed it as a means of weakening the secular PLO.) Sharon's deliberate provocations at a site sacred to both Jews and Muslims introduced an explicit religious dimension to the conflict for the first time.

Israel shows no signs of making peace either with its own history or with the Palestinians. The country's ultra-nationalists have for several years been pursuing a very different goal: the recognition of Israel – especially by the Palestinians – as a *Jewish* state. In November 2014, the cabinet proposed legislation to declare Israel a 'Nation-State of the Jewish People' and to abolish Arabic as the second official language.

This may seem paradoxical – after all, who could see Israel as anything other than a Jewish state? – but there are concrete political calculations at work. These are to do with demographics: there are already more Palestinians than Jews between the Mediterranean and the Jordan River. Israel, *de facto* in mid-annexation of the West Bank, will not be able to avoid indefinitely the question of what is to be done with them. What if they were to drop their demand for a state of their own, and instead begin to insist on equal rights with the citizens of 'Greater Israel'?

In order to prevent this, the nationalists need the Palestinians to recognise Israel as a 'Jewish state'. The domination of the Jewish minority over the Arab majority would then be permanently enshrined, nothing more than a legitimate exercise of state (or 'Jewish state') power. Effectively, the colonial power is demanding that the 'natives' agree to the removal of their rights. Even the British Empire wouldn't have come up with this idea. The outcome will be a form of ethnocracy. The story of Apartheid in South Africa is one of violence, injustice, and ultimately failure; the Middle Eastern version is not likely to be any different. Yet the alternative, the two-state solution, today seems little more than a fading memory of an old dream.

The Israel-Palestine conflict increasingly plays out on the religious level. Though it occupies only a tiny area of land, the Temple Mount has become a symbolic point of contention. Jewish extremists demand the right to pray on the grounds of the Al-Aqsa Mosque. They are supported by Israeli politicians, who simultaneously restrict Muslim access to the site. The right to prayer is likely to be just the first step; next will be a formal division of the Temple Mount, as has already happened at the Tomb of Abraham in Hebron. One half for the Jews, the other for the Muslims. And then why not rebuild the Second Temple, destroyed by the Romans, which stood exactly where the Al-Aqsa Mosque stands today? Indeed, this was already being advocated in the 1980s by right-wing extremist Rabbi Meir Kahane, among whose supporters was the man who assassinated Prime Minister Rabin in 1995. The plan is: first replace democracy with a theocracy (or a religio-ethnocracy), then repress or (ideally, if possible) expel all Palestinians.

Jews versus Muslims – where will that lead? Netanyahu sets Hamas on a level with Islamic State, just as Sharon equated them with al-Qaida. This is little short of inviting a jihad against the Jewish state. Events at the Al-Aqsa mosque could spark just this, and become a symbolic rallying-point for Muslims. The worst-case scenario: Islamist groups around the world declare the fight for Jerusalem a religious duty, and the conflict in Palestine becomes still more bound up with the violence in Syria and elsewhere. If Jewish and Muslim extremists were to jointly set the region aflame, no possibility can be ruled out. What if there were a major attack on Israel, a country with nuclear weapons at its disposal?

A NEW WORLD ORDER

Does Middle Eastern history between the fall of Mossadegh in 1953 and the Israel-Gaza conflict in 2014 have any lessons to teach us? Most obviously, there is the gaping chasm between the freedom repeatedly promised by Western democracies, and the blood-soaked reality engendered by decades of military intervention and economic strangulation – to say nothing of the dictators buttressed by the West as long as they toe the line.

States have collapsed. New movements have formed, some of them terroristic. Meanwhile the Arab-Islamic world tried to shed its skin and set forth for new shores, before being blasted off course by a storm of near-apocalyptic violence. Did the West help during this time? Did we support the fledgling forces of democracy? We know the answer, of course. The US and its European allies have pursued a dual agenda that has nothing to do with freedom or democracy: we have striven to secure our own access to oil and gas, and we have helped Israel to extend its stranglehold over the people of Palestine (though naturally we prefer to speak in terms of Israel's 'security'). Daniel Barenboim, the pianist and conductor who unites Israeli and Arab musicians in his orchestras and at his academy in Berlin, has suggested that America 'could solve the conflict in three days by exerting pressure on the Israeli government.'[36] Can we honestly say that we think he is wrong?

The conflicts in the region are coming thicker and faster, and

---

36 Maria Santececilia. Interview with Daniel Barenboim/'The World Is Suffering From A Lack Of leadership'. www.qantara.de. 24 November 2014.

they are more and more global in their reach. There was an interval of 26 years between the fall of Mossadegh and the Iranian Revolution: an age from our contemporary perspective. Only five years ago, few had heard of Islamic State. What the Middle East will look like in another five years is anybody's guess. Already Syria and Iraq have ceased to exist as nations, except on maps. Will governments and states fall across the entire Middle East, as they did in the former Yugoslavia?

Certainly, the traditional Western levers of influence – armies and sanctions – will not be able to stop this happening. They have been tried and tested, and they have failed. New ideas are needed, but Western thinktanks do little other than churn out the same old doom-laden observations about the downfall of the liberal world order, or the half-hearted way in which the US plays its role as the world's policeman. They forget that the world has only ever been 'liberal' to a lucky few. The inhabitants of Gaza or Baghdad, Afghanistan or Libya have scant reason to shed tears over America's twilight of the Gods. And lest it be forgotten, it was the self-same policeman who helped to create the enemies of today's world. Al-Qaida and Islamic State both deserve the label 'Made in the USA'.

In retrospect, the global 'winners' did not make use of the historic opportunity that the fall of the Berlin Wall in 1989 afforded. The American political philosopher Francis Fukuyama wrote at the time of the 'end of history'. The phrase itself has long passed into history, yet it does seem to epitomise the blindness of the West. The notion that Western-style capitalism and democracy had triumphed for all eternity, that the market would rule in all its beneficent glory until the end of days, was never anything but narcissistic folly.

The world is not the same as 'the West' – the handful of

Anglophone countries plus continental Europe and Japan whose imperial ambitions have wrought centuries of havoc on all continents. There was a chance to reset relations with Russia, the big loser from the collapse of communism, to found a new politics of mutual respect with other countries, to acknowledge the many victims of Empire. Instead, the West chose a different path: the pursuit of total dominance. Yet even as NATO expanded eastwards, China's economic rise became unstoppable, and Russia re-appeared as a global player. Brazil, India and South Africa emerged as more and more powerful economic presences. They will not let Washington call the shots for ever.

Meanwhile the world appears in a state of permanent unrest. At the turn of the century, the US still believed in the paradise known as the New Economy: growth and prosperity through technological innovation, along with peace on Earth due to the progressive growth and enrichment of the global middle classes. But the financial crash in 2008 was followed by recession, stagnation and high unemployment in Europe. Convictions faltered, certainties and securities vanished. Little is permanent except change, and that does not promise the dawn.

We are living in an age of growing confusion and complexity, and no single power will bestride it. The era of global hegemony, from the twin dominance of the USA and the USSR after 1945 to the post-1989 supremacy of America and its allies, has had its day. China's arrival on the world stage does not mean the old game will continue, only with a new omnipotent player. Even if it wanted to, Beijing couldn't rise to hegemony.

Multi-polarity is the essence of today's world, with its proliferation of power centres both old and new. Among these are nations and groups of nations, global businesses like Google or Amazon, secret services, political movements, non-state actors, global criminal or terrorist networks, and non-governmental organisations. They jostle for power and influence in an ever-shifting environment; are friends today, foes tomorrow.

This convoluted – not to say chaotic – new terrain demands diplomacy, efforts at cross-cultural communication, and pragmatism. It is by no means clear that those who currently hold power or dictate opinion in the West have understood the signs of the times. Instead, they lose themselves in the minutiae of day-to-day politics, and insofar as they consider the bigger picture, cling to their simplistic division of the world into 'good' and 'evil'. In doing so, they overlook the fact that most people live at the mercy of forces over which they have no control, without rights and with no hope of attaining anything remotely like our privileged existence. These people have lost, and they know it. Often enough, they react to the iniquities of a world order formed by the West with violence – which, of course, is why the West labels them as 'evil'.

The idea that there is such a thing as a Western 'community of values' rests on much-cherished beliefs. One is that the dominance of the West came about, not through power and violence, but through a kind of evolution in which Western civilization, based on understanding and reason, represented the end-point of a Darwinian process. Inexplicably, though, our version of liberal democracy has failed to reproduce itself all over the world. How can it be that the Russians still love their Putin, the Turks their Erdogan, when both lead authoritarian states?

In truth, there is no great mystery. In emerging economies, the lower and middle classes aspire to what we in the West already have: a consumer society, shored up by a welfare state. Freedom of opinion is less important to them than their own advancement; their ideal is often the 'doer', the strong man, who has climbed from nowhere all the way to the top. In many such regions, rules and world-views based on patriarchal ideas and an authoritarian interpretation of religion and nationhood are still very much the norm.

Besides, the people of the Middle East have paid dearly for believing in the West's promises of freedom; they have witnessed the evisceration of their states and the deaths of hundreds of thousands of their fellow human beings. They also know that a great many Europeans and Americans view Islam with hostility and contempt – and that fundamentally different standards are applied to Israel than to everyone else.

The Indian historian Pankaj Mishra puts it like this: 'Only the most hopelessly self-satisfied people will today claim that the Western way of life is the best one and that the rest of the world should copy it with the help of nation building and capitalism of Western design. In this unsettlingly diverse and fast world, dogmas that lump everyone together are no longer wanted.'[37]

It is essential that other cultures and nations are permitted to decide their own path. For our part, we must decide where we fit into a new, more confused and confusing world, not just in a political sense, but also in matters of culture and identity. According to a Chinese saying, when the winds of change blow by, some build walls, and others build windmills. These closing words plead the case for windmills. Let there be no division of the world into 'us' and 'them'. Today's great fault lines do not run between states, religions or ideologies; they run between groups who are fighting for power and resources. There is no 'war of cultures'; there is a war over the global honeypot. Most victims of radical Islam are Muslim, not European or American, even if we

---

37 Pankaj Mishra 'Das Westliche Gejammer' (The West's Lament). *Die Zeit.* 13 September 2014

tend to sit up and pay attention only when they look like us or when terror shows up on our own doorstep.

My own people, the Germans, are world champions at remembrance, but like other Europeans we find it hard to accept that the West can do serious wrong. Injustice is something perpetrated by others: by Russia, China, Muslims... They're the ones who oppress and murder. The war in Vietnam, the putsch against Mossadegh, the invasion and occupation of Iraq: few and far between are the 'transatlantic' politicians who would dare to put these publicly in the same category.

Values are part of the DNA of Western society. They help shape its identity, and to legitimise its actions. It is precisely because these values have genuine value that they must not be allowed to deteriorate into political buzzwords, mere smoke screens that hide self-interest behind noble-sounding sentiments. If human rights play no role in relations between the US and Israel, are not invoked over Gaza or Guantanamo, but form the battle-cry whenever Western powers wish to attack opponents such as Putin or Erdogan, then they have become mere verbal husks, with morality playing second fiddle (if at all) to sheer expediency.

Let us start with small steps. Let us not rely on politicians or journalists mired in outdated provincial outlooks. Let us take responsibility ourselves, be conscious of our many privileges. Let us learn to be humble and modest regarding the achievements of our own culture. The sooner we realise that millions of people in the Middle East alone are simply trying to survive, the easier it will be to stand by them. Especially those who come to us as refugees: let us help them put down roots, here because they will stay. Let us outlaw both anti-Semitism and Islamophobia. Let us stubbornly resist those who are trying to abuse our freedoms. This includes all those who have sown the wind and reaped whirlwinds, not just in the Middle East, foremost among them George W. Bush, Dick Cheney, Tony Blair and Donald Rumsfeld. Only when these men, these great architects of ruin, face criminal prosecution the International Court of Justice in The Hague will the promise of a 'Western Community of Values' have truly delivered.

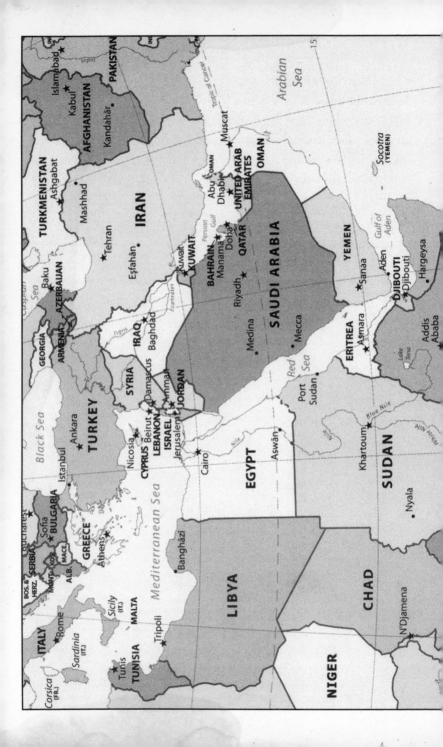